Penetrating Wisdom
The Aspiration of Samantabhadra

Penetrating Wisdom

THE ASPIRATION OF SAMANTABHADRA

The Dzogchen Ponlop Rinpoche

▼

SNOW LION PUBLICATIONS

ITHACA, NEW YORK • BOULDER, COLORADO

Snow Lion Publications
P.O. Box 6483
Ithaca, NY 14851 USA
(607) 273-8519
www.snowlionpub.com

Printed in USA on acid-free recycled paper.

ISBN-10: 1-55939-266-5
ISBN-13: 978-1-55939-266-2

This book is based on teachings given at Theksum Tashi Choling,
Hamburg, Germany in December 1996 and Nalandabodhi, Boulder,
Colorado in July 1998.

Library of Congress Cataloging-in-Publication Data

Dzogchen Ponlop, Rinpoche, 1965-
 Penetrating wisdom : the aspiration of Samantabhadra /
by the Dzogchen Ponlop Rinpoche.
  p. cm.
 ISBN-13: 978-1-55939-266-2 (alk. paper)
 ISBN-10: 1-55939-266-5 (alk. paper)
 1. Rdzogs-chen. 2. Samantabhadra (Buddhist deity) I. Title.
 BQ7662.4   D96 2006
 294.3'420423—dc22

                                        2006017466

Designed and typeset by Gopa & Ted2, Inc.

❧ Contents

❧ Editor's Foreword

Penetrating Wisdom is a commentary by The Dzogchen Ponlop Rinpoche on "The Aspiration of Samantabhadra." As the Seventh Dzogchen Ponlop, Rinpoche is a direct spiritual heir to these teachings. He received transmission of this text from His Holiness Dilgo Khyentse Rinpoche. Rinpoche's tremendous scholarship and direct understanding of these teachings enables him to communicate both the words and the meaning of this Aspiration Prayer. As such, his teaching is a precious gift of the Dzogchen lineage directly to us.

It is our great privilege to have this book published and to assist Rinpoche in bringing these teachings to a wider audience. This commentary was given in two series of talks to his students in Germany and the United States. The commentary gives the text a living quality, enabling readers to see its application in daily life. Rinpoche's use of colloquial English, along with his precise translations of both Sanskrit and Tibetan terms, gives invaluable insight into the meaning of the text.

For ease of reference, each section begins with the verses of the root text on which that portion of the commentary is based. When specific lines of the root text are referenced within the commentary, they are again included in italics. Both Tibetan and Sanskrit terms are rendered phonetically in the text. As much of Rinpoche's commentary uses Tibetan terms and translations as a foundation, we have chosen to use primarily Tibetan for clarity and continuity.

The Glossary includes terms in English, Sanskrit, and Tibetan. Tibetan terms are presented in the original script, their Wylie transliteration in brackets [ ], and a phonetic rendering in English in parentheses ( ). In those cases where Rinpoche has not specifically defined a term in the commentary itself, the Glossary includes a general explanation. Where indicated by "NG," the definition is taken from *Mahamudra—The Ocean of Definitive Meaning*, by the Ninth Gyalwang Karmapa, Wangchuk Dorje, ©2002 Nitartha *international*. These definitions are used with the kind permission of Nitartha *international*.

It is a daunting task to edit a commentary like this. We have undertaken it at Rinpoche's request. To the extent that errors have crept in, these are entirely the fault of the editor.

The fruition of this project could not have come to pass without the efforts and dedication of many of Rinpoche's students, both transcribers and translators. Many thanks and much appreciation goes to all of them.

However, first and foremost, we are indebted to Rinpoche for his kindness and clarity in presenting these teachings. We dedicate whatever merit may result from the publication of this book to the long life and continual expansion of Rinpoche's activities, which will doubtless benefit all beings.

❧ The Aspiration of Samantabhadra

HO

All that appears and exists, all of saṃsāra and nirvāṇa,
Has one ground, two paths, and two results.
It is the display of awareness and ignorance.
Through the aspiration of Samantabhadra
May all be fully awakened
In the citadel of the dharmadhātu.

The ground of all is uncomposed,
An inexpressible, self-arisen expanse
Without the names "saṃsāra" and "nirvāṇa."
If it is known, buddhahood is attained.
Not knowing it, beings wander in saṃsāra.
May all beings of the three realms
Know the inexpressible ground.

I, Samantabhadra,
Know naturally that ground
Without cause and condition.
I am without the defects of superimposition and denial of outer
*   and inner.*
I am unobscured by the darkness of mindlessness.

Therefore, self-appearance is unobscured.
If self-awareness remains in place,
There is no fear even if the threefold world is destroyed.
There is no attachment to the five desirables.
In self-arisen, nonconceptual awareness
There is no solid form or five poisons.
The unceasing lucidity of awareness
Is five wisdoms of one nature.
Through the ripening of the five wisdoms
The five families of the first buddha arose.
From the further expansion of wisdom
The forty-two buddhas arose.
As the display of five wisdoms
The sixty blood drinkers arose.
Therefore, ground-awareness never became confused.
As I am the first buddha,
Through my aspiration
May beings of saṃsāra's three realms
Recognize self-arisen awareness
And expand great wisdom.

My emanations are unceasing.
I manifest inconceivable billions,
Displayed as whatever tames beings.
Through my compassionate aspiration
May all beings of saṃsāra's three realms
Escape the six states.

At first, for bewildered beings
Awareness did not arise on the ground.
That obscurity of unconsciousness
Is the cause of bewildered ignorance.

From that unconsciousness
Emerged terrified, blurry cognition.
Self-other and enmity were born from that.
Through the gradual intensification of habit
Sequential entry into saṃsāra began.
The five poisonous kleśas developed.
The actions of the five poisons are unceasing.
Therefore, since the ground of the confusion of beings
Is mindless ignorance,
Through the aspiration of myself, the buddha,
May all recognize awareness.
The connate ignorance
Is a distracted, mindless cognition.
The labeling ignorance
Is holding self and other to be two.
The two ignorances, connate and labeling,
Are the ground of the confusion of all beings.
Through the aspiration of myself, the buddha,
May the thick, mindless obscurity
Of all samsaric beings be dispelled.
May dualistic cognition be clarified.
May awareness be recognized.

Dualism is doubt.
From the emergence of subtle clinging
Coarse habit gradually develops.
Food, wealth, clothing, places, companions,
The five desirables, and beloved relatives—
Beings are tormented by attachment to the pleasant.
That is mundane confusion.
There is no end to the actions of dualism.
When the fruit of clinging ripens,

Born as pretas tormented by craving—
How sad is their hunger and thirst.
Through the aspiration of myself, the buddha,
May desirous beings
Not reject the longing of desire
Nor accept the clinging of attachment.
By relaxing cognition as it is
May their awareness take its seat.
May they attain the wisdom of discrimination.

Through the emergence of a subtle, fearful cognition
Of externally-apparent objects
The habit of aversion grows.
Coarse enmity, beating, and killing are born.
When the fruit of aversion ripens,
How much suffering there is in hell through boiling
    and burning.
Through the aspiration of myself, the buddha,
When strong aversion arises
In all beings of the six states,
May it be relaxed without rejection or acceptance.
Awareness taking its seat,
May beings attain the wisdom of clarity.

One's mind becoming inflated,
An attitude of superiority to others,
Fierce pride, is born.
One experiences the suffering of disputation.
When the fruit of that action ripens,
One is born as a god and experiences death and downfall.
Through the aspiration of myself, the buddha,
May beings with inflated minds

Relax cognition as it is.
Awareness taking its seat,
May they realize equality.

Through the habit of developed dualism,
From the agony of praising oneself and denigrating others,
Quarrelsome competitiveness develops.
Born as an asura, killed and mutilated,
One falls to hell as a result.
Through the aspiration of myself, the buddha,
May those who quarrel through competitiveness
Relax their enmity.
Awareness taking its seat,
May they attain the wisdom of unimpeded activity.
Through the distraction of mindless apathy,
Through torpor, obscurity, forgetfulness,
Unconsciousness, laziness, and bewilderment,
One wanders as an unprotected animal as a result.
Through the aspiration of myself, the buddha,
May the light of lucid mindfulness arise
In the obscurity of torpid bewilderment.
May nonconceptual wisdom be attained.
All beings of the three realms
Are equal to myself, the buddha, in the all-ground.
It became the ground of mindless confusion.
Now, they engage in pointless actions.
The six actions are like the bewilderment of dreams.
I am the first buddha.
I tame the six types of beings through emanations.
Through the aspiration of Samantabhadra,
May all beings without exception
Be awakened in the dharmadhātu.

A HO
From now on whenever a powerful yogin
Within lucid awareness without bewilderment
Makes this powerful aspiration,
All beings who hear it
Will be fully awakened within three lives.

When the sun or moon is grasped by Rāhu,
When there is clamor or earthquakes,
At the solstices or at the year's change,
If he generates himself as Samantabhadra
And recites this in the hearing of all,
All beings of the three realms
Will be gradually freed from suffering
And will finally attain buddhahood
Through the aspiration of that yogin.

From the *Tantra of the Great Perfection Which Shows the Penetrating Wisdom of Samantabhadra*, this is the ninth chapter, which presents the powerful aspiration which makes it impossible for all beings not to attain buddhahood.

Translated by Lama Yeshe Gyamtso and The Dzogchen Ponlop Rinpoche.
© 1998 by Lama Yeshe Gyamtso and The Dzogchen Ponlop Rinpoche

PART ONE

Faith

❧ Aspiration Prayer

"THE ASPIRATION OF SAMANTABHADRA" belongs to the Dzogchen tradition of Vajrayana Buddhism. It comes from the primordial buddha Samantabhadra, known in Tibetan as Kuntuzangpo. Fundamentally speaking, this prayer is the aspiration of the dharmakaya buddha Samantabhadra.

In addition to being the prayer of a primordial buddha, it is a prayer of the path to complete awakening according to the Dzogchen tradition as well as a prayer of instructions that make our path more genuine and correct. It is a prayer that expresses the different manifestations of rigpa, which is our basic awareness, in ordinary life. Further, it is a prayer and aspiration for the realization of rigpa, the realization of the genuine path, and the realization of the genuine teacher.

It is said that many Dzogchen tantras descended from space onto the rooftop of the king's palace in Uddiyana. Later on, these tantras were taught by the sambhogakaya buddha Vajrasattva to the great human master of Dzogchen, Garab Dorje. From Garab Dorje, it came to Manjushrimitra and Shri Simha. From them, it came to Padmasambhava and so on. I received the transmission of this text from His Holiness Dilgo Khyentse Rinpoche and the transmission of this tantra from Tulku Urgyen Rinpoche. Briefly speaking, that's our lineage.

This presentation is based on the commentary by the Fifteenth Gyalwang Karmapa, Khakyap Dorje. In that way, the presentation becomes more authentic.

As this is very much a Vajrayana prayer, it is necessary that we have a genuine ground for making such an aspiration. My teacher gave me very important instructions concerning this ground. He said it is faith, faith without any questions. It is devotion and trust in the inconceivable truth. That is the ground of Vajrayana practices such as this.

Believe it or not, faith is the basic requirement for us to enter the path of Vajrayana, to enter the paths of Dzogchen or Mahamudra. It is a sense of complete trust without much distraction. It is faith, trust, and confidence in the basic ground of inconceivable truth, in the reality beyond concept. Even if you don't have complete faith and trust, it is important to have some sense of openness to the possibility of a reality beyond concept, beyond ordinary perceptions.

In our day-to-day life, we get totally enveloped in the reality that we experience through our low-tech sensory perceptions. We believe in our six sensory perceptions, which include concepts. We believe that the highest degree of truth is something that we can see, something that we can hear, and something that we can feel. We take them as the ultimate authority. We reject everything that is beyond our ordinary perceptions. The biggest obstacle in the path of Tantra, in the paths of Vajrayana, Mahamudra, and Dzogchen, is completely and utterly trusting these ordinary perceptions. The truth is out there and it cannot be experienced by these low-tech perceptions.

Our modern scientific culture has a very strong dogma of not believing in a reality beyond our perceptions and concepts. But even from the modern scientific point of view, our sensory faculties are quite low-tech. We see the coarse elements of existence with these faculties, but when we look at them through the scientific technology of a microscope and so forth, we don't find the same reality. In modern physics, it is seen as some kind of energy field, like a quark. Our sense faculties are not able to experience that level of subtlety, let alone inconceivable reality.

We usually rule out the possibility of inconceivable reality. We rule it out because we cannot perceive it with our samsaric sense organs. We say, "Because I can't perceive it, I can't believe in it." If something doesn't fit the logic of samsaric confusion, the logic of the self-centered view of egocentricity, then we rule it out. We can't conceive of the inconceivable truth with our samsaric thoughts. These are very strong obstacles to our understanding Vajrayana.

Not everything we learn on the Vajrayana path is necessarily completely conceivable or completely perceivable. In order to understand Vajrayana, we need to have some faith in the inconceivable truth. Even if we cannot have one hundred percent faith and confidence, just leaving some space for that possibility is a good start. Therefore, the first important quality on the path of Vajrayana is the quality of faith. We need a sense of openness, at least, to the possibility of nonconceptual reality or inconceivable truth. This faith, which is the enlightening thought of the possibility of the inconceivable truth, is the basic ground to have a flash of awareness.

Usually, people think only of faith in the deity or faith in the lama, but that is not the basic meaning of faith here. The basic meaning here begins with faith in this inconceivable truth. In Vajrayana, that is the fundamental faith. Therefore, I think it is important to share this very helpful advice and instruction that I received from my Vajra master. It is very important to share it with all of you interested in the Vajrayana journey.

This faith in Vajrayana is not like the conventional sense of confidence. Conventionally, you can apply some logic from a conceptual thought frame. But samsaric logic has no value in Vajrayana faith. So long as you remain in that samsaric logic, the Vajra path does not become very stable. So long as samsaric logic is still the ground for our faith, our Vajra path is not particularly established. Therefore it can be difficult; it can be tricky. That is the very challenging beginning of a Vajrayana journey. I think Westerners like challenges, so here we have a great opportunity!

❧ Vajra Master

W HEN I TALK ABOUT the Vajrayana guru, I usually say it is like the movie *Judge Dredd*, where he says, "I am the law." There is no trial, no jury. It is just straight to execution. In many cases, that is what the Vajrayana guru says. I am not here to discourage you, but I have to speak the truth. It is a pretty claustrophobic situation that is extremely dangerous and scary.

The Vajrayana master plays a very important role in terms of developing this sense of faith. That is because Vajrayana faith begins with our trust, confidence, and faith in the teacher who is our guide on the spiritual path, and in the lineage that holds the wisdom of such path. It is trust and faith in the fruition of the path as well as in the teachings that lead us to the fruition of enlightenment. In other words, it is having the sense of positive mind that says, "There have been many lineage masters in the past. There are many lineage masters living at present. Yes, this leads to fruition."

Faith in the inconceivable truth begins with our faith in the lineage, with our faith in the Vajrayana path, and with our faith in the Vajra masters. The reason we rely on the Vajra master is that we have already tried many different methods to wake ourselves up, but none of them really worked. We set our alarm clock for the next morning and then, in the morning, it beeps with a very unconfident beep. It beeps because we have ordered it to beep, but its beep is very feeble. It has a very weak quality because it knows that it doesn't have the full power to wake us up.

When this feeble beep happens, our great samsaric command is to move a hand with tremendous habitual power and press the snooze button. Then we go back to our comfortable samsaric sleep. We go back again to the dreams and nightmares to which we are attached. Fifteen minutes later, the alarm clock beeps again. Again, we press the snooze button. We don't have this faith, this confidence in the inconceivable truth that can wake us up. This goes on for ages, maybe kalpas after kalpas. That's why the Hinayana and Mahayana journeys take so long.

There is a logic in the ordinary kind of waking up process. When you set the alarm, you choose when it will beep and how loud it will beep. At the same time, you have the choice not to wake up. It is very logical.

The Hinayana and Mahayana journeys can be very logical. They may work more closely with the samsaric mind and gradually take you step by step beyond samsaric logic. But Vajrayana goes beyond logic. This is a very important point. Vajrayana is like asking someone to wake you up in the morning. You are not relying on an alarm clock. You are relying on this person, the Vajra master, to wake you up.

You really need great faith in this person and great faith in his method of waking you up, because there is no logic. You don't know how he or she is going to wake you up, that's for sure. You need a great sense of openness because you must hand him the key to your apartment. Otherwise, there is no way that he can enter your space to wake you up from your samsaric confusion.

The process of handing over the key is what we call devotion, what we call openness. The trust and faith that we are talking about here is like handing over your key. After that, it is totally up to the Vajra master as to the methods he or she will use to wake us up. It will definitely not be an alarm clock. The most civilized method that a Vajra master might use to wake us up would be a bucket of ice-cold water. After you get that kind of wake-up call, you won't have any second thoughts of going back to sleep because your samsaric bed is no longer warm and snug. It is a horrible wet bed with a wet blanket. All you can think of is to get up, just simply to wake up. There is really no other option left.

You can see from this analogy that the Vajrayana method is very strong. It is very striking, very awakening. At the same time, it may not be a very pleasant or comfortable method for our ego. Therefore, it requires tremendous faith in the Vajra master and in the Vajra lineage. That faith is the key to our awakening. I am emphasizing this because it seems that there is no result produced through any path or any practice without this faith. For that reason, the lineage principle is very much emphasized in the Dzogchen tradition.

When you have faith at the beginning, it may be conceptual or theoretical. To a certain degree, if you one-pointedly concentrate on devotion, on trust, and on faith, it goes beyond concepts. Then you one-pointedly meditate and it becomes a nonconceptual experience. Once you concentrate one-pointedly, it will become a naked experience.

There is a story about a teacher called Gendün Chöpel. He was a great Tibetan teacher in the twentieth century. At a certain point, he was acting a bit crazy. One of his students offered him chang, which is Tibetan beer. He was drinking and they were discussing dharma. The student was one-pointed in his devotion and trust. He was one-pointedly concentrating on each and every word of his teacher, no matter what he was saying. At a certain point, the student felt a little bit drunk. He wasn't drinking at all, but he felt a little bit drunk. He also smelled alcohol on his own breath. Then he sort of came back to his conceptual world and, of course, nothing was there.

When he explains this story in his biography of Gendün Chöpel, the student says that he felt for a moment that he was in the state of his guru's mind, like merging as one. He even had the outer signs of feeling a little bit drunk and smelling alcohol on his breath. But the main thing he felt was actually the mind of the guru, which of course you can't speak or write about in any particular way except to describe the outer signs, symbols, and feelings that he had.

This story shows that by one-pointedly putting your faith in this person, or in these teachings, there can be some kind of nonconceptual experience. In the Vajrayana journey, we call that merging your mind with the mind of the guru. There's a sense of a merging through devotion and faith, which is definitely connected to confidence and trust. It is not just blind faith that we are talking about here. Devotion involves wisdom and knowledge.

With that devotion and faith, we are willing to take this journey to the other side of the suffering known as samsara, to the great bliss that is known as nirvana. It is the same as passengers who must rely on the ferryman, or on the pilot, for their journey. It is the same idea. It really requires tremendous trust. When you board a plane, you are completely putting your trust in the people in the cockpit. We usually don't think about that. We just walk onto the plane without much thinking. If you really think about it, you are putting tremendous trust and confidence in those few people in the cockpit. Your life is in their hands.

For example, I myself don't know anything about how to fly the plane. It is beyond my concept to fly the plane, but I put my trust in the pilot. In a similar way, we are putting that same kind of trust in our Vajra master. We are putting that same trust in the Vajra lineage, the Vajra boat, the Vajra plane, the Vajra rocket. And with that trust, that faith, we take the journey on the Vajrayana path.

❧ Lineage Principle

IN THE VAJRAYANA, lineage is the most important principle of the journey. Vajrayana was not created in Tibet by some trippy Tibetan masters or in India by some crazy Sadhu. It was taught by Lord Buddha Shakyamuni and by great buddhas in the past. It was kept alive in India by many Vajra masters, called the Mahasiddhas, and then it came to Tibet. There, it was kept alive by the great Tibetan Mahasiddha yogis.

How was the Vajrayana kept alive? It was kept alive through the pure transmission of the lineage, the continuity of enlightenment that has been given down from master to student. The Vajrayana path does not exist without transmission, which does not come from a book or from a person alone. It comes from the enlightened heart, the enlightened realization.

The manner in which the pure Vajrayana transmission is transmitted and how it is received has never been institutionalized. It is transmitted individually on a very personal basis. Therefore, it has the quality of freshness. In that way, the transmission meets the needs of an individual practitioner in his or her own style of receiving such transmission. That's the most important point here.

Vajrayana depends a lot on interdependence, known as *pratitya samutpada* in Sanskrit. These little interdependent arisals are important in Tantra, particularly in the beginning. Even great masters like Marpa, Milarepa, and Naropa relied on such methods.

It's not just important in the outer sense. For example, Milarepa came looking for Marpa and found a man plowing his field. So Milarepa, not knowing it was Marpa, asked this person he had found, "Where is this teacher called Marpa, this very famous teacher called Marpa, the great translator?" Marpa answered, "I don't know about that famous teacher, that great translator, but there is a family person called Marpa in that house." He pointed at the house and said, "If you help me plow this field, I'll go and see if he is available. If you get tired, here is beer that you can drink." So he left one jar of chang, and the rest of the field to be plowed.

Then Marpa went inside the house and never came out. Milarepa plowed the whole field very well and drank the whole jar of beer. This seems very ordinary, very unimportant. But later Marpa said, "That was a great coincidence and very auspicious. Plowing the whole field means that you will be very diligent in your practice and that you will cut through every obstacle. Drinking the whole jar of beer means that you will receive the complete transmission of what I have." So you see, two seemingly ordinary and unimportant things can be very important in Tantra. You can never tell what is not important. Only the Vajra master can tell.

Some people may need a slap on their forehead for transmission or else the teachings may not work. If a person really needs a slap on his forehead, then the right guru should know. He should also know that such person won't sue him in the future. In our lineage, Tilopa took off his flip-flop and whacked Naropa's forehead. Naropa fell unconscious for awhile and then, when he got up, he was a completely realized person. Therefore, transmission is the key on the Vajrayana path, and especially in the Dzogchen tradition.

Some of the key instructions are simple, such as when Gampopa was leaving Milarepa. You can read about it in their biographies. It was the last time they would be together so it was a very sentimental situation. They couldn't let go of each other so they went on together further and further and further. Finally, Milarepa said, "OK, now let's stop here. You go on your journey but, before you leave, I have a very profound instruction that I haven't given you before." He pulled his pants down, showed Gampopa his bum, and said, "See this?" Milarepa's bum was completely hardened with calluses from sitting in meditation on the rocks. Milarepa said, "That's the last and most profound instruction." Transmission is very nice.

Some instructions are that simple. Others go on and on for years and years and years of teaching. Through confidence in our lineage masters, our lineage teachings, and our lineage Sangha of the enlightened beings, we can develop this faith and trust in the inconceivable truth.

Vajrayana is very different from the New Age approach. The difference is that the Vajrayana teachings are controlled by the lineage. I know we don't like the word "control," but the Vajrayana teachings are actually held by the authority of the lineage. I know we also don't like the word "authority," but we have it in Vajrayana. When we have this pure lineage, this genuine lineage, there is no space for our egocentric interpretation of dharma. We cannot interpret dharma like the New Age gurus. We cannot invent a new lineage because a lineage must be received. It must be received by transmission. It is not something we can just create here. That would be New Age, probably from California.

The Vajrayana lineage controls our ego-centered interpretations of dharma. We are not denying that there is an individual understanding of dharma, an individual way of hearing, contemplating, and meditating dharma. There is individual understanding of dharma. However, there is a big difference between individual understanding and individual interpretation. That is why Buddha taught three yanas.

Although Buddha gave many teachings, we only hear what we want to hear. For example, if we want to do just one practice of Mahayana, we only listen to the teachings on Mahayana that we want to hear. If our teacher has taught us Mahayana teachings that we don't want to hear, and wants us to practice them, we totally deny them. We interpret them in different ways and don't practice them. This is a serious problem for us.

When we can individually hear and practice dharma, that is our Vajrayana style. But when we individually interpret dharma, then we are going outside Vajrayana. I don't know where we are going at that point, but it's not Vajrayana.

⚛ Guru-Disciple Relationship

T HE GURU-DISCIPLE RELATIONSHIP is a very critical issue on the Vajrayana path. We must not get into the Vajrayana path until we are certain about it. Once we get into it, we should not mess up too much. That's a very dangerous game to play.

The best way to control our dangerous journey is to analyze your guru in the beginning as much as you can. Analyze, examine, and work with great diligence. Then, come to a conclusion. It will not be that dangerous if your conclusion is based on a good analysis in the beginning. These are some tips to be aware of on the Vajrayana path.

The method used to analyze the qualities of a Vajra master has been described in the Vajrayana lineage teachings. Briefly, the first quality of a Vajra master is that he keeps his vows. This means that he keeps them pure, whether they are Hinayana, Mahayana, or Vajrayana precepts. The second is that he has received the full empowerment and transmission of the Vajrayana lineage from his master, who has the lineage. It is not like receiving it from a New Age guru. Rather, it is receiving the lineage from an authentic teacher who has that lineage. Third, a Vajra master is one who has kept the samaya with his guru perfectly. In other words, one who has not broken his commitment with the guru. Finally, a Vajra master is one who has tremendous compassion, which means being nonaggressive and nonmilitant. These are the major qualifications.

A Vajra master is also one who has experience in what he is teaching. He is not someone who just digs up lots of books in the library, puts some things together, and goes to the lecture with many note cards, which then become a teaching. It is not like that. Rather, he teaches from what he has received from his master, what he has practiced, and what he has realized or at least experienced. That's what we call a good master.

The basic Buddhist intellectual approach is a very good basis for analyzing the master, the path, and the practitioner. If we analyze with that balance of the intuitive mind and the intellectual mind, then there is no doubt that we will find the right path and the right teacher. But if we get carried away into an extreme by either one of them, then it becomes a really big problem.

The proper way to follow the Vajrayana path is to first develop faith. Having developed faith, we can then jump into this path, into this journey. Therefore, as preparation for practicing the Vajrayana path, we must reflect on our own heart, our own basic practice, and our own basic understanding of dharma. We must reflect on our understanding of the teacher, the teachings, and the path. Through this reflection, we can develop this confidence, this trust, and this faith.

Sometimes we may misunderstand and say there is no space at all in the Vajrayana for any kind of doubt. That's not true. It is very very dangerous to say that we must not have any doubts! Buddha said doubt is wisdom. He said that inquisitive mind is wisdom. We are more than welcome to have doubts and inquisitive mind about the path and practices. At the same time, we must not go so far with these doubts that we get caught up and carried away by them.

It is very important for us to reflect on the nature of our path as well as what we are doing on our path. Reflect on how it is a Vajrayana, Mahayana, or Hinayana path. Reflect on how we face obstacles in practice. It is especially important to reflect on the teacher-student relationship.

It is important for us to reflect on what we expect from our teachers. Then we can see how much we project unnecessary things onto them. We can see how we fantasize about our teachers and make them look like a bronze statue, a carved African mask, or whatever. It's not true! Our masters in the past were all humans. Those living in the present are all humans. Shakyamuni Buddha was a human prince. He was an Indian guy, which we often forget. We think of him as a glowing golden statue, a beautifully carved wooden statue, or a stone statue, but that's not true. That's not who he was.

It's very important for us to see clearly that our teachers are human beings. They're all on the path to enlightenment. The historic Buddha is different, he's already enlightened, but the rest are all in the same boat. The only difference is that there may be different levels of realization; some are on the tenth bodhisattva bhumi, some are on another of the bodhisattva bhumis. Some may be on an ordinary bhumi.

We must see very clearly what we really expect from our teachers and what we really need. We must see what we expect in terms of guidance on the Hinayana path, guidance on the Mahayana path, or guidance on the Vajrayana path. We should reflect on that and then just be simple. We are looking for a path and for instruction on that path. That is what you get from most teachers, I hope. We should appreciate what we get. If we don't get enough of what we really need from our teachers, we should look for more. It is very important for us to reflect on these things and be grounded, so to speak. Then our path becomes more fruitful because everything is much simpler. It is more naked and honest.

As we discussed, selective hearing of the teachings is one problem. Selective guru is another problem. We jump from one guru to another. Why? Because one guru may be getting a bit too strict, going a little against our ego, our kleshas, and our emotional interests. When that happens, we don't like that guru anymore and we jump to another one. We try to find somebody who will tell us that what we want to do is correct, that it is Vajrayana.

These problems of selective practice, selective hearing, and selective guru become our major obstacles on the path. They are why we cannot perfect our path. We are stuck in this deep samsaric swamp of poverty mentality. We are stuck in dissatisfaction, which was our fundamental reason for joining the dharma. We bring the same dissatisfaction onto our dharma path, and say, "No, this teaching is not good enough, this dharma is not good enough."

Do you know the saying that the grass is always greener on the other side of the fence. Another version is that the other lane is always moving faster. These things are not necessarily happening outside: it is human psychology. We call this "dissatisfaction," or "poverty mentality." Buddha said that this is the basic suffering of human beings.

We should not bring this outlook onto our dharma path. It becomes a big obstacle to hearing and practicing Vajrayana dharma. In Vajrayana dharma, you cannot simply switch your guru overnight and still attain enlightenment in this lifetime. It is not possible. If you try it, Vajrayana becomes a very difficult path.

I want to be honest. I want to discourage your fantasies and misconceptions of Vajrayana. I want to discourage the neurotic pattern that you bring onto the Vajrayana path, which is that same neurotic pattern of dissatisfaction, of poverty mentality. I am not saying that you are the only one to bring this with you. We all do.

When we are infected by a serious disease and we go to a genuine doctor, that doctor will tell us frankly, "You have been infected by such and such disease." Of course, no one likes to hear that. It is very painful. The doctor may say, "It is very difficult to cure." We certainly don't want to hear that. We would like the doctor to say, "No, it is not a big problem. It is just a flu. I can cure this in one hour if you take such and such a pill."

It is the same with gurus. If we go to a genuine teacher, it's very painful. It was very painful when my teacher told me, "You have to do one hundred thousand prostrations." It was very painful and, obviously, I didn't like it. I wished that I could get another teacher who would tell me, "You just do one prostration and you will be enlightened." But that was not the case.

If we go to some trippy false doctor, that doctor might say, "No problem, I'll cure you in five seconds." Maybe he will say that he can cure us in one hour, or perhaps three months. We go through the whole treatment. We spend our money, our time, our energy, and we are still sick. Finally, we end up going back to the original genuine doctor. We end up going back to him because these false doctors cannot cure our disease. Sooner or later, we realize it's not working. It's just a fantasy. We have to go back to the painful fact that we have been infected. We have to go back to the painful fact that it is not easy to cure. We have to go back to the painful fact that we have to go through difficult treatments, such as surgery.

It is the same with the dharma path. The fact is that we have been infected by the disease of egocentricity. When we go on a genuine path, with a genuine master, it is not a simple and easy quick-fix. That is the fact. We have to come back to reality. With faith and confidence, we have to be more focused on the lineage principle and follow the painful instructions of the guru. That's the only way we can cure our disease of ego. Is that enough discouragement? I think so. Well, there is always Prozac, the drug that makes you happy.

Question: It sounds like I just need to trust, but what about my critical intellect?

Rinpoche: First, you must be critical, very much so. You must examine and analyze your guru. You must examine and analyze your path. You must examine and analyze the lineage. That is very important. Through examining and analyzing, critical mind should come to some trust, some faith. Critical mind needs a sense of limitation, which is based on a certain trust and faith. Buddha said that if you let your critical mind go on forever, then it might lead you to paranoia.

At the same time, this doesn't mean that you cannot ask questions. It means that your critical mind becomes an inquisitive mind. The inquisitive mind is very much emphasized by Buddha. When your critical mind has come to certain conclusions of trust and confidence in Vajrayana, that becomes faith. Then you continue your journey with that faith. You can still have a lot of questions and challenges. There is no problem there. The basic point is that we should not lose this faith in the inconceivable truth.

Q: Faith has always been very difficult for me. How can I work with that?

R: Fundamentally speaking, in order to awaken oneself in the state of realization, we need determination. We need willingness. We need the faith or trust in our own heart, in the path, and in realization. Without that faith, it's not going to take place no matter how hard we try. It's like people who talk about going to Nepal for 20 years but don't really make up their minds to go. They never get there. Maybe they say they want to go because everyone is talking about going, or everyone has been there or something, but they are not really determined to go.

PART TWO

Dzogchen

❧ Great Perfection

THIS ASPIRATION PRAYER comes from the Dzogchen tantra called the *Tantra of the Great Perfection Which Shows the Penetrating Wisdom of Samantabhadra*. In Tibetan, the short title of this tantra is *gongpa sang-thal gyi gyü*, which means "The Tantra of Penetrating Wisdom" or "The Tantra of Transcendent Intention." In English, the prayer is entitled "The Aspiration of Samantabhadra." It comes from the primordial buddha of the Dzogchen lineage known as Samantabhadra in Sanskrit, and Kuntuzangpo in Tibetan. Kuntuzangpo is the buddha of dharmakaya enlightenment, the enlightened body of truth.

"Dzog" means "to perfect" or "to complete" as well as "to exhaust." "Chen" means "great." So, Dzogchen means "great perfection," "great completion," or "great exhaustion." It is a state of being totally free. At this stage, you have exhausted every tiny bit of ego-clinging, every element of emotional disturbances. Therefore, it is called "great exhaustion." It is also called "the great completion" because in that state, all the wisdom of buddha is complete, all the elements of enlightenment are complete. There is nothing missing in this state. Finally, because your mind has never been polluted, it has always been in this state of complete purity. Therefore, it is called "the great perfection."

To convey fully the meaning of Dzogchen in English, the expression "full stop" is quite good. Full stop. Period. This period is a little but very powerful dot called the full stop. There is the sense of being full in that this dot has a circular form that is complete and full. At the same time, everything stops here: it doesn't go beyond this period.

Dzogchen has a similar meaning. On the one hand, it has this meaning of fullness, which is why we use the term "completion." It also has this meaning of stopping, which we express as exhaustion. Your whole expression of samsara has been exhausted, so it stops right here. It does not go beyond this. Therefore, Dzogchen is a giant full stop. This simple dot, this period called "full stop," has a very interesting meaning. So from now on, whenever you see a "full stop," remember Dzogchen!

The Dzogchen lineage originated from the dharmakaya buddha called the Kuntuzangpo Buddha. When we look at the thankgas, the painted images, you usually see the Kuntuzangpo Buddha on the top of Guru Rinpoche. Sometimes you see the Kuntuzangpo Buddha alone, sometimes you see him embraced with his consort, called the Kuntuzangmo, in union. Kuntuzangpo looks exactly like Shakyamuni Buddha in terms of shape and features, but he is blue in color, naked, and without any ornaments or clothing. He is completely naked reality.

The primordial buddha Kuntuzangpo actually taught the Dzogchen tantras. He transmitted these teachings without any words to the sambhogakaya buddha Vajrasattva. From Vajrasattva, they came to the nirmanakaya vidyadhara, the human Vajra master called Garab Dorje. Garab Dorje was born in the northeast of India, in Uddiyana, the birthplace of Padmasambhava. In Uddiyana, there was a great dharma king named Ashoka. He lived much earlier than the Ashoka we usually think of that built the stupa in Sarnath. This king Ashoka had a daughter, a princess called Prahadhani.

The princess was practicing celibacy. Once, while she was bathing in a beautiful lake, a beautiful white swan came and touched her heart with his beak. Later, she had some visions. Afterwards, it was obvious that she had become pregnant. Perhaps this inconceivable story rings a bell. Remember, I laid the ground earlier about the inconceivable truth.

The princess gave birth to a beautiful son. However, because it was an immaculate conception, she thought the child must be a very bad demon. So she threw the baby into the garbage. This often happens in our world as well.

The baby survived in the garbage for forty-nine days. Not only did the baby survive, but it was luminous and beautiful. Therefore, they decided that the child must be something special and they nourished him. This little child became Garab Dorje.

Garab Dorje was the first human master of the Dzogchen lineage, the first human holder of the Rigpa tradition. He received the transmission of all the Dzogchen tantras and teachings directly from the sambhogakaya buddha Vajrasattva. Garab Dorje transmitted the whole lineage to his heart son, Manjushrimitra, an Indian yogi. Manjushrimitra transmitted the lineage to Sri Simha, a Chinese yogi who lived in India. From Sri Simha, it was transmitted to our famous master Guru Padmasambhava.

If you look at how these transmissions took place, it's quite amazing. For example, when Sri Simha transmitted the lineage to Padmasambhava, it is said that he reduced Padmasambhava to the size and form of the syllable ༀ (Hūm). Padmasambhava became the syllable Hūm. Sri Simha took this Hūm, put it on his tongue, and swallowed it. Then Padmasambhava came out from the other end. At that point, he had received the full transmission of Dzogchen. He received the full realization and the full experience of Ati Yoga. This is what we call inconceivable! I think this is also sometimes called crazy.

Sri Simha also transmitted the lineage to both Vairochana and Vimalamitra. Later, these three masters, Padmasambhava, Vairochana, and Vimalamitra, came to Tibet. They brought this Vajrayana lineage transmission called Dzogchen to the Tibetan soil. They planted this teaching in the land of Tibet, in the culture and language of Tibet. From then on, we have had the continual lineage transmission of the Dzogchen tantras, including this "Aspiration of Samantabhadra."

With that lineage and transmission, this aspiration is very much connected to Dzogchen practice and teachings.

Vajrayana is also called the Secret Mantrayana. It is kept secret because there is the possibility of misunderstanding. There is the possibility of misleading oneself on to the wrong path, which is a path that goes against our motivation for liberation. Therefore, it is kept secret and taught between one Vajrayana master and one Vajrayana disciple.

Sometimes Tantric teachings are known as self-secret. They are not necessarily hidden by someone. They are called self-secret because the language of Tantra is secret, the symbolism of Tantra is secret, and the practice of Tantra is secret. If you read the Tantra, it's hard to understand. If you look at the iconography, what does it mean that these buddhas have animal heads? It is secret. Similarly, if you try to do Tantric practice, it is secret. We sleep every night, but it has never become a practice for us. We have dreamed so many times in our life, but it has never become a practice for us. In Tantra, it is practice. It is self-secret practice. That secrecy has to be revealed by what we call the transmission lineage.

Basically, all tantras are protected by the dakinis. Sometimes it is not very easy to receive their permission. As this is a democratic country, you may be able to get this book from an ordinary bookstore so anybody can read it. But that doesn't mean you are reading it in a Vajrayana sense. Just simply knowing how to explain some words doesn't mean we are actually teaching Dzogchen. Just simply meditating on some deities doesn't mean we are meditating on Dzogchen tantra.

What I mean by permission is this Secret Mantrayana permission. It is permission for us to openly speak, to practice, and to realize. I am not talking about little beautiful beings called angels. I am talking about dakinis; that's different. Therefore, I hope we have permission to read and practice such teachings.

❧ Five Aspects

THE PRAYER BEGINS with its title, "The Aspiration of Samanta-bhadra." In Tibetan, Samantabhadra is translated as Kuntuzang-po. "Kuntu" means "completely," "utterly," or "purely." "Zangpo" means "good" as well as "gentle." So, Kuntuzangpo means "completely pure," "completely good," or "completely gentle." Kuntu-zangpo also means "utterly pure," "utterly good," "utterly gentle," or the nature of our mind. It is all good, all excellent. It refers to our basic purity, the basic state of phenomena that is completely free. It is the basic state of all phenomena. It is the basic state of all our living experiences. That state is referred to as Kuntuzangpo. It is also what we call the primordial buddha.

The primordial buddha called Kuntuzangpo is completely pure, completely free, and completely good. It is our basic nature of mind, our fundamental state of being. That state of being Kuntuzangpo is very much inside. It is very much outside as well. When you look up in the sky, you find that same purity, that same state of goodness and freedom, that same principle of Kuntuzangpo. In a similar way, when we look at any place outside, we find that same state of purity. There-fore, Kuntuzangpo is the basic nature of all phenomena.

There are five different aspects of Kuntuzangpo. These are five dif-ferent ways to understand the nature of the utterly pure, all good, all excellent state of phenomena. The first aspect is called the Tönpa Kun-tuzangpo. *Tönpa* means "teacher," one who shows the path, one who shows the nature of mind, one who shows the nature of phenomena. This refers to the Kuntuzangpo Buddha who shows us the path and who is in this ultimate state that is completely pure and completely good. The Teacher Kuntuzangpo provides us with the clarity and precision of teaching that makes all phenomena appear as the Tönpa Kuntuzangpo.

This first aspect of Kuntuzangpo is the Samantabhadra Buddha himself, the teacher. It is the dharmakaya teacher that manifests in the sambhogakaya and as nirmanakaya buddha. All of those are called the Tönpa Kuntuzangpo, the teacher, who is primordially pure, gentle, good, and completely free from any fabrications. The first aspect of Kuntuzangpo is the primordial buddha, which is the enlightened master.

The second aspect of Kuntuzangpo is called the Gyen Kuntuzangpo. "Gyen" means "ornament" and "Kuntuzangpo," as before, means "completely pure." Ornament Kuntuzangpo refers to the dharma teachings that the enlightened masters show on the path of enlightenment. These are like the teacher's ornaments or attributes. In most cultures, ornaments are usually worn around the neck. They are connected to the neck or throat, which, in some sense, is a kind of speech center.

The nature of the teachings is also utterly pure, utterly good. If we were to go into details, then we could talk about different kinds of teachings that are all good, all excellent. So the translation "all good" works very well. It shows that the teachings, the words that we are taking as the path or as instructions on the path, are also in that same nature of primordial enlightenment. Therefore, the words are not simply words: they are the essence of enlightenment.

It is through words that we often get transmission. Through words, we get enlightened instructions. Through words, we communicate with enlightened beings, the nirmanakaya buddhas. So the words, the teachings, are in the nature of primordial buddha that is the awakened state. The teachings are as pure as the basic state of the Tönpa Kuntuzangpo, the completely pure buddha. This is the second aspect of Kuntuzangpo, the Gyen Kuntuzangpo.

The third aspect of Kuntuzangpo is called the Lam Kuntuzangpo. "Lam" means "path." The Path Kuntuzangpo refers to the path of Dzogchen, which means that the path is completely pure, good, or excellent, right from the beginning. Not only are the tönpa, the teacher, and the gyen, the ornaments or attributes, pure and complete, but the path is pure and complete as well. This means that the path is not the cause. In Dzogchen, the path itself is fruition. Therefore, this path is completely pure, genuine, and good. It is in the state of Kuntuzangpo.

The Vajrayana path is known as the path of fruition because we are not working with causes to produce the result. Instead, we are taking the result as the path. That's why it's a very powerful journey. Kuntuzangpo is in every state, starting from shamatha at the beginning all the way to shamatha at the end. Therefore, this path is in the nature of a primordial awakening.

That leads us to the fourth aspect of Kuntuzangpo, Rigpa Kuntuzangpo. What we are trying to realize on the path is rigpa, which is naked awareness or bare awareness. That bare naked awareness, rigpa, is in the state of Kuntuzangpo. It is primordially pure, completely pure, utterly pure, and is called the Rigpa Kuntuzangpo.

The first three Kuntuzangpos concern the teacher, the teachings, and the path. Rigpa Kuntuzangpo refers to the practitioner. Rigpa is the nature of our mind, and the nature of our mind is rigpa. Therefore, the primordial buddha is not outside us. The primordial buddha is within us, within our mind. When we talk about rigpa, that's the basic state of enlightenment. Therefore, it doesn't matter whether it's at the level of fruition of a Kuntuzangpo Buddha or at the level of path as a practitioner. This naked awareness is the same nature of the Kuntuzangpo Buddha and the practitioner Kuntuzangpo.

Rigpa has the quality of sharpness as well as the quality of genuineness. In genuineness, there is nothing pretentious. It is beyond makeup, so we get to this level of nakedness. For that reason, there's a saying in the Dzogchen literature, "The happiness Kuntuzangpo or the suffering Kuntuzangpo." Happiness is utterly pure and suffering is utterly pure. In the ultimate space of Kuntuzangpo, there are no differences between happiness and suffering, just as there are no differences between inside and outside. It is all in the same expanse of the great perfection called Kuntuzangpo. This state of Kuntuzangpo is the fundamental state of all phenomena, whether it is outside or inside, whether it is suffering or happiness, whether it is emotion or freedom from emotion. In Dzogchen, they are all in the state of Kuntuzangpo.

The nature of mind of all practitioners on this path of Dzogchen is in the nature of this bare awareness, rigpa, the primordial state of buddhahood. In other words, rigpa is the realization we are trying to accomplish. Therefore, the fourth aspect of Kuntuzangpo is the Rigpa Kuntuzangpo, the nature of mind.

The fifth aspect of Kuntuzangpo is called the Togpa Kuntuzangpo. Togpa is realization. Togpa Kuntuzangpo is the realization being completely pure, primordially pure. The realization of this primordial awareness, which is the ground, is a fruition state. It's a primordial experience as well as a primordial realization. This means that our realization of the Rigpa Kuntuzangpo is nothing new.

We have the idea that we will achieve something new after a certain amount of practice. According to the Dzogchen teachings, this realization has been with us all the time, primordially. That's why it is utterly pure, a primordial realization. Therefore, it is Togpa Kuntuzangpo, which is the absolute result.

You can look at Kuntuzangpo in these five different ways. This aspiration prayer, called "The Aspiration of Samantabhadra," comes from these principles of Kuntuzangpo, the primordial buddha. We are aspiring to accomplish this state of Kuntuzangpo.

❧ Recognizing Rigpa

OUR MIND IS PRIMORDIALLY in the state of rigpa. Whatever state of mind we go through, whether it is a very heavy experience of ignorance or a very outrageous emotion of anger, we have never moved from the state of rigpa. Our mind has always been in the state of rigpa, but we don't realize it all the time.

When we don't realize it, there is no continuity of the experience. The nonconceptual experience of rigpa, the flash of the wisdom of rigpa, is constantly interrupted. That interruption is what is called "covering." Realization is when we totally overcome that interruption so that the experience becomes one continuity.

In more Mahamudra terms, Milarepa said that between two conceptual discursive thoughts, you experience nonconceptual wisdom. There is a moment of nonconceptual wisdom in between thoughts. We don't realize that, we just miss it all the time. We are pretty good at missing it.

Once we have a flash experience of rigpa, we gain a deeper faith and confidence in this path, in this teaching, and in this realization. Then it's not a theory anymore, it's a firsthand experience. While that flash experience may just happen to some people, normally it doesn't. That flash experience comes from the pointing-out that you receive from your own teacher, your own guru. Then, you will have certainty. When we get that from a Vajra master, and really experience it first hand, it is beyond guessing. We don't say, "Oh, maybe I got it, maybe not." There is no guessing needed because it is direct.

In the Dzogchen tradition, it is through combining our devotion, which is our trust and confidence in this inconceivable rigpa and in the lineage masters of rigpa, with the transmission called the rigpa pointing-out empowerment that we experience a flash of rigpa. This doesn't mean that our experience of rigpa won't be interrupted from then on. If we nurture that flash, which has been given birth in our mind, it can be developed into a full-grown youthful experience of rigpa.

The actual nonconceptual state of our experience of rigpa comes from devotion. We could say that the experience of rigpa is the realization of the guru. When we put our confidence, devotion, and trust in our guru, when we listen to his instructions and totally click into that state of instruction, then we experience the naked nature of rigpa. Therefore, devotion plays an important role in experiencing rigpa.

Devotion, in some sense, can be taught. It can be explained the way compassion is explained. We talk first about dualistic compassion. Dualistic compassion is seeing someone suffering, therefore you feel compassion. That leads us to the state of ultimate compassion, the compassion of the buddhas, which is nonreferential and beyond duality.

Similarly, we could say there is a conceptual aspect of devotion and, at the same time, there is a nonconceptual aspect of devotion that is generated through a conceptual devotion. At a certain point, if your confidence begins to manifest greater mindfulness, greater awareness, then with the process of devotion, confidence manifests fully and completely. That fullness of the manifestation of confidence may not be any different from the experience of rigpa. Ultimately, what you have confidence in is rigpa, the Kuntuzangpo nature. That's what you are realizing.

The method in Dzogchen or Mahamudra is not complex, it is very simple. The main thing is to recognize your own true nature of mind. For that, there is a simple meditation in Dzogchen and a simple meditation in Mahamudra. The main thing is to look inside, not to look outside. Then you will realize. That's how it works. That's why it is called simple.

It is said in both Mahamudra and Dzogchen, "Because it's too close, we don't recognize it." It is like our own eyes, which cannot see themselves. Gampopa said, "Because it is so simple, we don't believe it." If I just tell you, "It's so simple. Look at your mind, that's buddha!," it's hard to believe, hard to get.

One problem with our human mind is that we like complexity, we are addicted to it. When someone presents something with a lot of complex formats, we think it's very profound. If it's very hard to understand, it must be very profound. But if it's something very easy, we say, "Oh, it's too cheap." That's exactly what Gampopa was saying. Because it is so simple, we don't believe it.

It's the same thing in modern society. For example, if you teach dharma in modern society with a pure motivation, without accepting any donations or charging anything, they will say, "Oh, that's fishy! Maybe he is trying to propagate something. Maybe he is trying to sell something, some propaganda." But when somebody charges an outrageous amount for a weekend, like with New Age groups, thousands of people go. They think it is profound because it is so expensive.

Sometimes our mind really works just as Gampopa says. If it's too easy, we don't believe it. If it's too close, we can't recognize it. Therefore, the complex path has been created by our own mind. Don't misunderstand me, I have no hard feelings toward New Age groups. When I used the New Age example, I was not saying it's totally wrong or bad, I am just trying to clarify the Vajrayana by pointing out these differences. That's all.

Question: Is there a difference between rigpa and Kuntuzangpo?

Rinpoche: We can understand the difference by examining the five Kuntuzangpo principles. For example, rigpa is inseparable from Rigpa Kuntuzangpo, but it is slightly different from Togpa Kuntuzangpo. Togpa Kuntuzangpo is the uncovered state of rigpa. When we talk about rigpa within our heart, within the minds of sentient beings, we are speaking about rigpa that is temporarily covered. It is in the state of Rigpa Kuntuzangpo, but it has not yet become Togpa Kuntuzangpo. While they are basically the same, rigpa in sentient beings is more of a potential. It is the basic state that has not yet been revealed completely.

Q: Why is all this taught as being so simple, when doing it turns out to be so difficult?

R: Look at the many stories of the Mahasiddhas. They didn't get it the first time. They didn't get it the second time. There were many times that they didn't get it. For example, when Naropa received teachings from Tilopa, he didn't click into it right away. It took some time. Finally, Tilopa got fed up. He took off his sandal and, with his full strength, hit Naropa on the forehead. Naropa almost went unconscious. At that point, he got it. The method is simple whether it takes a long time or a short time.

The practice is simple. It is as simple as the teachings on emptiness. But why has it become so complex? Why is Madhyamaka so irritatingly complex? It's because our conceptions are that complex. It's because the things that need to be transcended are so complex. Therefore, the Madhyamaka, Dzogchen, and Mahamudra teachings may appear to be complex because of what we need to reject.

It is our approach that is making the teaching complex, the teaching itself is not. Madhyamaka is very simple and straightforward: it just says shunyata. Dzogchen is straightforward and simple: it just says rigpa. If you realize rigpa, then you are buddha. If you don't realize rigpa, then you are a confused sentient being. That's Dzogchen.

Mahamudra says the same thing. If you realize ordinary mind, *thamal gyi shepa*, you are a buddha. If you don't realize ordinary mind, you are a confused samsaric being. To realize it, we have to cut through this net of conceptual hang-ups. For that, we need the complex Madhyamaka logic. If it doesn't work, then we have Mahamudra meditation. And if it still doesn't work, then there are the Dzogchen teachings.

Sometimes it doesn't work because of the complexity of the defilements. If that is the case, then the practice may appear to be complex. But in the basic sense, the teaching and the practice itself are very straightforward.

PART THREE

Fundamental Ground

HO

All that appears and exists, all of saṃsāra and nirvāṇa,
Has one ground, two paths, and two results.
It is the display of awareness and ignorance.
Through the aspiration of Samantabhadra
May all be fully awakened
In the citadel of the dharmadhātu.

The ground of all is uncomposed,
An inexpressible, self-arisen expanse
Without the names "saṃsāra" and "nirvāṇa."
If it is known, buddhahood is attained.
Not knowing it, beings wander in saṃsāra.
May all beings of the three realms
Know the inexpressible ground.

⊰⊱ Basic Purity

W E BEGIN WITH the aspiration of the basic purity of samsara and nirvana. It is the aspiration to realize the basic state of samsara and nirvana as being in one genuine nature. It begins with "HO." Ho is an expression of nondual speech. In Tibetan, we call it *jö tu me pay jö pa*, which means speechless speech. Ho is also an expression of surprise, an expression of nondual joy. It comes from the same root as E MA HO. You may have heard E MA HO or A HO before in the Vajrayana literature. They all express this basic sense of the wonderfulness of certain experiences, such as when you experience joy or when you experience naked rigpa within your fundamental hatred. It expresses the fundamental delight that sometimes comes with a particularly shocking experience. These words are said by yogis to express this sense of appreciating that particular wonder.

The fundamental experience of joy or delight does not necessarily manifest with a smooth experience of path. It could also manifest with the experience of your hatred, jealousy, passion, aggression, or pride for that matter. Ho expresses the basic state of satisfaction, which is another leap beyond the dissatisfaction that is our fundamental state of samsara.

After HO, comes the first discussion of the ground:

> *All that appears and exists, all of saṃsāra and nirvāṇa,*
> *Has one ground, two paths, and two results.*

"All that appears" refers to the container that is our samsaric existence. It refers to our group experience of shared karma, which is the common experience of different realms. The container is fundamentally the same to all of us. You see this as paper, I see this as paper. Similarly, we both experience seeing the beautiful Colorado Rockies as amazing, especially at sunrise. That's a common experience to all of us.

"Exists" refers to the contained beings in the various realms, such as the human realm, animal realm, and so forth. As with our group karma, beings in each of the different realms experience a common world. For example, the sentient beings that live in water have a common experience of the realm of water, whether they live in oceans, lakes, or rivers. The sentient beings that primarily manifest in the sky have their common experience of living in the sky. That fundamental or basic experience is what we call "All that appears and exists."

The container and contained include all of samsara and nirvana, all experiences of samsara and all experiences of nirvana. Samsara is not recognizing our basic nature. It's also a perfume from France. Basically, samsara is experiencing phenomena through ego-clinging. When you experience anything through ego-clinging, there is the experience of samsara. Samsara is nothing more than that.

Nirvana is the absence of suffering and pain. Nirvana is also a rock band. Nirvana is the experience of the basic nature of mind, which has the quality of freedom and spaciousness as well as the experience of basic goodness that is the nature of mind. It is the experience of ego-lessness, which is seeing things as they are.

Samantabhadra says that all of samsara and nirvana, meaning all confusions and all wisdoms, have one origin. They have one common ground from which everything arises. This common ground is also known as the basis. In Dzogchen, that basis performs the function of generating these two expressions called "samsara" and "nirvana." Both are generated and both appear from the same common ground.

Another way to understand this one ground is that there is one origin for both Sutrayana and Vajrayana. Again, that's why it is called one basis. The fundamental basis of the ground for both Sutra as well as Tantra is the basic shunyata, the primordial emptiness. According to the Dzogchen and Mahamudra traditions, that ground is the alaya nature of our mind. So, one ground here refers to all experience manifesting from the same fundamental state. That primordial alaya is inseparable from the Mahayana understanding of shunyata. It is inseparable from the Mahamudra view of ordinary mind.

The one fundamental ground is seen in two different ways. It manifests as the all-basis consciousness, alayavijnana, or the all-basis wisdom, alayajnana. In the study of buddha nature, there is a lot of discussion about alayavijnana and alayajnana. We relate to the one basic nature with two different approaches. With one approach, it becomes vijnana, consciousness. With the other approach, it becomes jnana, wisdom.

From the Dzogchen point of view, it is one basic mind stream. When you look at this mind, which possesses eight different consciousnesses from the Mahayana point of view, or six different consciousnesses from the Hinayana point of view, it's one continuity that manifests as a samsaric consciousness. Alternatively, the same eight bases manifest as five different wisdoms. Therefore, it is one ground. If you recognize it, it is wisdom. If you fail to recognize it, it is consciousness. It is that simple from this point of view. Therefore, the Prayer says,

> All of samsāra and nirvāṇa has one ground,
> two paths, and two results.

Samsara and nirvana are definitely two different paths. As we know, the path to samsara begins with ignorance and continues on the twelve links of interdependent origination, the twelve nidanas. That is very clearly the path to samsara. If you follow ignorance, the chain of thoughts leads us into the different emotional games and poisons on the path of samsara.

If you follow the path of nirvana according to Dzogchen, you go on the nine-yana journey. You begin with the Shravakayana and Pratyeka-buddhayana, which are the Hinayana; then the Bodhisattvayana, which is Mahayana; then the Tantric path of Kriya Tantra, Upa Tantra, and Yoga Tantra; and then the Dzogchen Tantras of Mahayoga, Anuyoga, and then finally Atiyoga. The nine-yana journey is the path to liberation, so far as Dzogchen is concerned.

In the nine-yana journey of the Nyingma Dzogchen teachings, it says that the ground is Madhyamaka, the path is Mahamudra, and the result is Dzogchen. The first three yanas are the Sutrayana, the ground. The highest view in Sutra is shunyata, which is Madhyamaka. On the path level, you have the outer, inner, and secret Tantras: Kriya Tantra, Upa Tantra, and Yoga Tantra. In these three yanas, the view is Mahamudra.

When you get to the last three yanas of the nine-yana journey, Mahayoga, Anuyoga, and Atiyoga, the view is Dzogchen. It is like ground, path, and fruition in a way. You can say that the ground is Madhyamaka, the path is Mahamudra, and the result is Dzogchen.

I taught this before and some Kagyupas got really upset. I think it is pretty strange, because they didn't think carefully. You cannot reach the result, no matter how high it is, without the path. You cannot get to the top of the skyscraper, no matter how high it is, without an elevator or staircase. No matter how important it is to have the penthouse type of view, you must rely on the foundations. You cannot have the penthouse without foundations. Without the ground, there is no path. Without the path, there is no result. That means they are equally important. People don't understand that and get very upset. They cling to the notion of result being higher. They get upset because they are so trapped in this samsaric nonsense of hierarchy. There is no point to getting upset. Ground, path, and fruition are equally important.

If you look at the path element in terms of the Sutrayana journey and the Vajrayana journey, it is quite different. In the Sutrayana path, we have the Hinayana and Mahayana methods. In Vajrayana, the Dzogchen path consists of various Tantric methods that are different from the Sutrayana methods. The basic elements of the path cannot be that different, but the methods used are quite different. Therefore, it is said that there are two paths with one ground, one origin.

There's a very interesting joke that I would like to tell you. Two masters of Mahamudra and Dzogchen were having a debate. The Dzogchen master said, "The Dzogchen is much more profound. It's the highest path and the highest yana. There is nothing above. If you practice in your sleep, you can attain enlightenment. If you practice while you are awake, you can attain enlightenment. Even if you don't practice, you will attain enlightenment if you have the karmic connection. So Dzogchen is much higher." Then the Mahamudra teacher said, "Well, that sounds very good, but the Mahamudra teachings talk about one instant. In one instant, if you recognize it, you attain enlightenment in that same instant. If you fail to recognize it, then you are confused. Therefore, Mahamudra pointing-out is much more powerful because you can attain enlightenment in one instant. You don't have to go to sleep to practice, you don't have to wake up to practice, and you don't have to hang around to attain enlightenment."

This prayer shows the same idea as the Mahamudra teachings of recognition in one instant. In any given moment, recognizing this all-basis consciousness is enlightenment. It is the five wisdoms of the Buddha. When you fail to recognize it, it is the eight or six consciousnesses, according to the Mahayana or Hinayana views respectively.

The two paths lead to the two different results of samsara and nirvana. There is the path of consciousness, which leads to the fruition of samsaric appearances and suffering, and the path of wisdom, which leads to the fruition of enlightenment that is the result of freedom from samsara.

In other words, there are two paths connected to the two different aspects of the alaya. The first path is called the alayavijnana, which does not recognize its own basic state, its own manifestations. The second path is the alayajnana, which recognizes its own face, its own manifestations. The path of alayavijnana, which does not recognize its own manifestation as its own nature, leads to the fruition of samsara. On this path, one is completely enveloped in a deeper and deeper cycle of duality. When we recognize our own display, our own manifestations, as the nature of alaya, it leads to the fruition of recognizing egolessness, the nondual nature of mind, wisdom, nirvana. Therefore, these two paths lead us to two different results.

For these reasons, many Dzogchen and Mahamudra masters say that the view and the teachings of Dzogchen and Mahamudra are closer to Shentong Madhyamaka. Shentong uses a lot of Yogacara terms like alaya, and so forth. There are many terminologies in common, so they feel much more comfortable teaching the Shentong view that relates directly to the paths of Dzogchen and Mahamudra.

It is the display of awareness and ignorance.

It is said in the prayer that both awareness and ignorance are a display. This display, this magical illusion, is called *chotrül* in Tibetan. With recognition, you get the magical illusion of nirvana. Without recognition, you get this magical illusion of samsara.

It is like an electric switch. If you turn it off, then you have darkness, ignorance. If you turn it on, then you have luminosity, recognition. It's just how you flip the switch. Here we are saying the same thing. If you recognize it and look in, it's called nirvana. If you fail to recognize it and always look out, then you are on the wrong side of the switch. It's very important for us to know this simple switch between samsara and nirvana.

If you look at the paths of Sutrayana and Tantrayana, the result is still said to be different. The enlightenment of the Sutrayana differs from the enlightenment of Tantrayana. The Hinayana path leads to the result of arhathood, which we call partial liberation. The Mahayana path leads to the full enlightenment of the Mahayana path. The Tantrayana path leads to the full enlightenment of the Tantric path.

Basically speaking, there is a difference in the result because Sutra and Tantra have different views in approaching the manifestation of the buddhas. In the Sutrayana approach, buddhas manifest in only three kayas. In Tantrayana, buddhas manifest in five kayas.

The basic difference is that the Sutrayana view of dharmakaya is complete emptiness, basic shunyata. Chandrakirti said very clearly in the *Madhyamakavatara* that when the continuity of any consciousness comes to cessation, that is dharmakaya. In the Tantric approach, dharmakaya is not just an empty state. It is not just cessation. Dharmakaya is the state of the inseparability of wisdom and space. The wisdom element is very important here. Dharmakaya is not just empty, it is full of qualities. It is full of the qualities of wisdom, yet it is in this nature of expansive space, which in Tibetan is called *long*.

So, with respect to Sutrayana and Tantrayana, the nature of dharmakaya is different. In the Sutrayana, the characteristic of dharmakaya has fallen a bit into the extreme of emptiness. In Tantra, there is the emphasis on the inseparability of space and luminosity. This inseparability is the union of the great expanse of shunyata and the full-of-quality luminosity, called "abhisambodhikaya." This union is the characteristic of dharmakaya in Tantra.

Because the characteristic of dharmakaya is different, the blessing is different as well. In the Sutrayana, dharmakaya manifests blessing in the two kayas of sambhogakaya and nirmanakaya. In Tantrayana, the blessing manifests in five kayas. It manifests in the dharmakaya, the body of truth, as the origin. The second kaya is the sambhogakaya, the body of enjoyment. The third kaya is the nirmanakaya, the body of manifestation. The fourth kaya is what we call the vajra body, the vajrakaya. The fifth kaya which is called the completely or thoroughly enlightened body, abhisambodhikaya. That's the difference between the dharmakaya of Sutra and Tantra.

There are two differences between Sutrayana and Tantrayana with regard to the sambhogakaya. Here, enjoyment refers to *yönten*, richness. In the Sutrayana, that richness is basically the enjoyment of positive actions and qualities. In the Tantrayana, sambhogakaya has the richness not only of the enjoyment of positive things, but also of transcending the negative things.

The second difference is the teaching method. The Sutrayana sambhogakaya teaches the Sutra methods to go beyond negative emotions. It teaches positive deeds, positive actions, and positive dharma. The Vajrayana sambhogakaya teachings include such good things as the paths and bhumis, but it also provides methods for dealing with our disturbing emotions. Our disturbing emotions are very strong and very difficult to deal with. The Vajrayana sambhogakaya is focused on and teaches the methods to transcend disturbing emotions. Therefore, there is a difference in the method of teaching.

Finally, there's a difference between the Sutrayana buddha of nirmanakaya and the Tantrayana buddha of nirmanakaya. The Sutrayana nirmanakaya buddha was the historic Buddha. The retinue of close disciples of Shakyamuni Buddha were those who had that fortunate karma. It consisted of those who had already somewhat purified their negative karma. Therefore, they could see the Buddha, they could be with the Buddha, and they could succeed on the path.

The retinue of the Tantric nirmanakaya buddha of Dzogchen is not always positive. It does not necessarily include only realized beings on the path. The retinue of the Tantric buddha is mixed with more disturbed sentient beings. That is why it is said that Tantra is very effective in this polluted time. Tantra becomes more effective because our mind is so polluted, so completely disturbed with emotions. For that reason, in the Nyingma tradition, many teachings have been hidden for centuries. Guru Rinpoche hid them in different places so that they could be discovered when our minds would become polluted. At that time, such teachings are beneficial. Therefore, the Tantric buddha not only benefits those with fortunate karma, it also benefits those with negative karma. Therefore, there's a difference at the end. That's why it says two results.

> *Through the aspiration of Samantabhadra*
> *May all be fully awakened*
> *In the citadel of the dharmadhātu.*

When the Prayer says, "Through the aspiration of Samantabhadra," it also means that we recite these verses from our basic purity. We recite them from our basic nature of mind that we call buddha nature, that is alpha-pure, and that is in the state of buddhahood, Kuntu-zangpo. By the power of that purity, that dharmata which is the essence of our nature, we make the aspiration that "all be fully awakened in the citadel of the dharmadhatu."

Dharmadhatu means the nature of phenomena. Generally, when we talk about dharmadhatu from the point of view of a subject-object relationship, it's more like the object. The wisdom of dharmakaya realizes the nature of dharmadhatu. Dharmadhatu is like the space of shunyata, which is realized by dharmakaya wisdom. Dharmakaya is usually referred to as wisdom, which can be further classified into *ji tawa*, the wisdom of seeing things as they are, and *ji nyepa*, the wisdom of seeing things in their varieties, to their extent.

In a similar way, there's a vajradhatu in Tantric traditions. Vajradhatu is the fundamental space of the vajra nature of mind. Dhatu means "space." In some sense, both dharmadhatu and vajradhatu have this sense of the union of ying and rigpa, which we call *ying rig tse* in Tibetan. There's also a vajrakaya, which is the fundamental kaya of enlightenment. Vajradhatu, that basic nature of all things, is experienced by the vajrakaya.

When we say, "Through the aspiration of Samantabhadra," we're not only thinking about the buddha, the dharmakaya Kuntuzangpo, but we're also thinking about the speech, the ornament of Kuntuzangpo; the path Kuntuzangpo, which we follow; the rigpa Kuntuzangpo, which is part of us; and the realization of Kuntuzangpo. With these, we aspire that all be fully awakened in the citadel of the dharmadhatu. That great space, that great nature of phenomena, is the palace where all samsara and nirvana perform their magical display. Our prayer is "May all be fully awakened in the citadel of the dharmadhatu." We aspire that all sentient beings realize this nature of awakened mind. Our aspiration is to realize that the display of rigpa appears as the forms of samsara or nirvana as well as that all sentient beings recognize their own display of the clarity nature of mind.

It seems to be necessary to have clarity in order to actually project duality. In other words, duality comes from failing to recognize clarity. For example, you need light in order to reflect in a mirror. In a similar way, you need light to project the negatives of film onto a screen in order to create that duality. From this teaching's point of view, our clarity nature of mind is so vivid and so intense that it manifests as subject/object duality to ordinary beings. When we recognize that the seemingly object nature of reality is nothing different than the subject nature of mind, which is rigpa, it is called enlightenment. When we see that truly and recognize that genuinely, we make this aspiration that all beings be fully awakened in the citadel of the dharmadhatu, the basic space in which the clarity is manifest.

❧ Ground and Fruition

THE NEXT ASPIRATION shows the relationship between ground and fruition. It shows that the ground of all is an uncomposed and inexpressible self-arisen expanse without the names "samsara" and "nirvana."

> *The ground of all is uncomposed,*

This shows the ground nature of samsara in relation to the fruition stage of buddhahood, which is enlightenment. From the Dzogchen point of view, the ground nature of all samsara and nirvana is uncomposed. This means that the ground itself is neither a cause nor an effect. The ground is not really a cause that produces the fruition of buddhahood. We are making a leap here from our basic studies of Hinayana and Mahayana to some kind of weird Dzogchen concept.

The ground we talk about here is the nature of mind. It is the ground of the nature of samsara and of nirvana. The nature of mind, the basic state of rigpa, has not been produced by any cause or condition. Therefore, that nature of ground is uncomposed.

There's a level of ground we talk about called *shönnu bum-ku*, youthful buddha in a vase. The youthful buddha is fully shining in that state of complete enlightenment. However, it does not manifest complete enlightenment because it is covered by the temporary veil of a vase. It is like a torch or a butter lamp inside a very thick container. When you open that container, the light fully manifests and whatever room it is in will be illuminated. The illumination is nothing new so far as the lamp is concerned. It has always been glowing.

In a similar way, buddhahood is not something new. It is not something newly realized or accomplished from the point of view of the ground. From the very nature of the ground, a full state of buddhahood manifests its complete qualities. Therefore, the Prayer says that the ground is:

> *An inexpressible, self-arisen expanse*
> *Without the names "saṃsāra" and "nirvāṇa."*

Here, "self-arisen" means the primordial state. It is not something we can fully express with words or concepts. It's beyond words or concepts. The nature of all is not biased; it is not restricted to one or another. The nature of all exists in one identical state. That ground, that nature, does not have any name such as samsara or nirvana. That is the foundation, that is the ground. It is beyond samsara and nirvana. Not knowing the ground means wandering in samsara. If you recognize this ground, if you truly experience this ground, buddhahood is attained. That is the fruition. That is the result of our practice and our path.

We call that one origin Kuntuzangpo, the primordial buddha in Dzogchen. It is also known as *kadak* in Tibetan. "Ka" means "alpha" or "primordial" and "dak" is pure, or purity. *Ka* is the first letter of Tibetan alphabet, so *kadak* means pure from the beginning. *Ka ne dag pa*, to make it a full word, means pure from the beginning, which is the state of Kuntuzangpo. It is the state of rigpa, which is the state of pure from beginningless time. That state of primordially-pure nature, the nature, is called emptiness or shunyata in the Mahayana. It is also known as freedom from elaboration.

The ground, that fundamental state of simplicity, is the origin of all elaborations. This pure basic state is like a simple artist's canvas. We paint different images on this canvas. We can paint the image of a buddha, and it becomes very pure, beautiful, and inspiring to look at. We can also paint a devil on the same canvas, which can create our fundamental suffering, our basic pain. However, the basis of both is the same simple state of canvas that is completely pure and totally free from the images we project on it. It is totally free, whether that image is a buddha or a devil. That is the origin.

The state of primordially pure nature, kadak, is not made by anything. It is uncreated. This means that the fundamental state of absolute reality, the basic ground, has never been compounded by causes or conditions. That nature of primordial purity, kadak, is beyond any elaboration. It is beyond conceptual formation, which means it is beyond philosophy. It is not created by any creator, outside or inside. It is not created by Kuntuzangpo nor was it created by any buddhas in the past. Therefore, whether we are talking about the nature of our mind or the nature of the universe, primordial purity exists in that nature. Both exist on that ground which is completely free from conceptual elaboration, primordially pure. That's why it is simple.

The primordial pure nature is spontaneously existing. When one recognizes that origin, that most fundamental state of Kuntuzangpo, one is called "buddha" or "one who has attained liberation, nirvana." When one misses that point and fails to recognize the primordial state of buddhahood, one slips into the samsaric ocean. Therefore, it is said that there is one origin for both samsara and nirvana.

So it is really not much different. The difference is between awareness and ignorance. Isn't it simple? Sometimes, teachers say that the basic teaching of Dzogchen and Mahamudra is as simple as this. Because it's so simple, people don't get it. Because our mind has this complexity of duality and ego-clinging, we make it more complex.

This shows that Samantabhadra attained buddhahood through the realization of this kadak, the alpha-pure nature of mind. The primordial buddha has seen and recognized that the nature of ground is free from causes or conditions. This is called the great way of liberation of the kadak nature of mind. The ground is free from the causes and conditions of any effort on the path as well as from conditions of fruition. Therefore, it is seen as the natural state of this great freedom called kadak.

Kadak exists in the form of this great expanse that is completely spacious. That spaciousness is called the spontaneously-arising expanse. It's part of the kadak, the alpha-pure. Alpha-pure does not just mean negation of impurity, of ego-clinging, or of emotional disturbances. There is some existence. That combination makes our ground balanced between emptiness and spontaneously arising luminosity. There is a union of the two in the state of kadak, alpha-purity.

Spontaneously-arising luminosity, *lhündrup*, is present right from the beginning. That's why it becomes an important issue to understand. So, that nature of kadak is not just in the state of being pure, empty, and free, but it is in the state of a spontaneously-arising expanse. It is not nonexistent. It exists in the state of primordial existence. That existence is not a creation. It's a spontaneous arising.

In Dzogchen, the wisdom that we are realizing on the path is there right from the beginning. It is existent right from the beginning, at the ground level. The ground of the kadak can be divided in many different ways, but the general division has three bases. The first is called the general basis, the second is called the basis of liberation, and the third is called the basis of confusion. So kadak is the basis of everything. It is the ground of both samsara and nirvana.

The ground has two wisdoms. First, it has primordial purity. That is the ground of primordial nature, the fundamental basis of our mind. It is the kadak. The second wisdom is lhündrup, which is spontaneously arising or spontaneously existing. These two wisdoms are the nature of our ground, which is inexpressible. These two wisdoms are something to be realized, something to be experienced. They are beyond words. All the words we use are simply methods to reach there, but the actual state of these two is beyond speech. If you think you are speaking completely about these two aspects of ground, then you are fooling yourselves.

In that nature of the inexpressible truth, the ground of kadak, the labels of samsara and nirvana do not exist. These labels are just conceptual. They are just discursive thoughts. The labels of samsara and nirvana do not exist in this fundamental nature because it is one ground.

So, samsara and nirvana both originate from the same ground of alpha-purity. That ground is spontaneously existing, which means kadak and lhündrup. At that primordial level, there is no separation between samsara and nirvana. There is no way that we can express and label these two as different things in this state of kadak and lhündrup.

If it is known, buddhahood is attained.
Not knowing it, beings wander in saṃsāra.

Kuntuzangpo says that when you have the pristine awareness to recognize that ground of suchness, then you are called enlightened. When we fail to realize that ground, when we ignore that state of ground and get fascinated by the labeling process of thoughts, we are called "beings wandering in samsara." Being fascinated by these magical illusions, by little magic tricks of ego, is called samsara.

Recognizing this ground is not just something that we discuss. It is not just something that we should listen to or that a speaker should speak about. It is something that we try to realize in our daily practice of meditation. It is something that we can think of achieving in our daily sitting practice, in our daily awareness. This is important to contemplate.

According to the Dzogchen tantras, as well as the Mahayana, ultimate reality is inexpressible. As Buddha emphasized in the Prajnaparamita Sutras, the nature of wisdom is beyond speech, beyond conception, and beyond expression. Forget about absolute truth and forget about the ground, we cannot even express by words the actual reality of relative truth. We can say some part of it, but we cannot really express our suffering. We cannot really express our joy. We can't even express our bittersweet experience of a chocolate. How can we express even that experience?

There is no way to express it, you know. We have to use an example to lead towards it, but the actual thing that we experience in our mouth, such as a piece of chocolate, cannot be expressed. We have to say that it is sweet, it has milk, and it has bitterness, like chicory. We have to use many different things to try to express one simple taste of chocolate. We can never say the actual thing.

This is the ground that we are trying to realize and toward which we are making the aspiration. Therefore, the Prayer says that the ground is an inexpressible self-arisen expanse without the names "samsara" and "nirvana." It is beyond samsara and nirvana. If we recognize this ground, that is buddhahood. Not knowing this ground means wandering in samsara. Since this is something to be realized, something we want to achieve, we make this aspiration prayer by saying,

> *May all beings of the three realms know the*
> *inexpressible ground.*

We are making the aspiration here that all sentient beings of the three realms recognize this inexpressible ground. Because it is the nature of their mind, it is the nature of their realm. As it is the nature of their world, they do not have to go out and search for this ground. It is wherever they are.

"The three realms" refers to the realm of desire, the realm of form, and the realm of formlessness. We belong to the realm of desire. There is no doubt about that. From the Buddhist point of view, the realm of desire includes the six realms: the hell realm, the hungry ghost realm, the animal realm, the human realm, the asura realm, and part of the gods' realm. The gods' realm is divided into the realm of form, in which the gods still maintain a certain aspect of form but mainly exist in samadhi, as well as the realm of formlessness, in which they do not have any physical form. They just exist in the realm of mental samadhi. Those are the three realms.

Ground itself, from the Dzogchen point of view, is actually fruition if you recognize it. We aspire that all sentient beings of the six realms attain this state of inexpressible ground.

Question: Does a student with a lot of problems in the beginning become a more effective teacher than one who didn't have to face many problems?

Rinpoche: Not necessarily. To be a good master really depends on your intention. If you have the very strong pure intention to dedicate your time and your energy to help somebody, you can help a lot of people even if you are not a great scholar.

There is a story about two great masters who wrote separate commentaries to the same text. Chandrakirti was a greatly respected master and a well-known scholar. Chandragomin was equally respected as a master but was not so well known as a scholastic conqueror. Chandrakirti is a great bodhisattva, so I cannot judge the truth of this, but the history says that he did not write his commentary with the pure motivation of helping, but rather with some scholarly pride. Chandragomin wrote his commentary with compassion, love, and caring for his students. He wrote it like a textbook. We no longer have Chandrakirti's commentary, it's been lost for a long time. No matter how good it was, we can't read it. But Chandragomin's still exists and we can still read it. So the saying is that when the motivation is pure, the benefit is greater.

Of course if we become a good teacher and have gone through a particular problem, we have more experience and more knowledge to help somebody going through that same problem. But if you have pride, it's not necessarily better.

Q: In what sense is nirvana still a magical illusion? I thought that nirvana should be beyond illusion.

R: It is not necessarily illusion, it is a magical display. A magical display can be illusion, but it's not necessarily illusion. What we are saying is that the nirvana we conceptualize right now as separate from samsara, and as something to be achieved, is another magical illusion. When we achieve the state of nirvana, it's actually not different from the primordial state. There is no separate state. When you think nirvana is something to be attained at the end, that nirvana is a magical display. It is still relative so long as we have the conception of nirvana. Even the display of sambhogakaya and nirmanakaya is the display of nirvana. That's what magical means. It's in the relative; it's not in the absolute.

Q: If we are faced with very destructive energy from ill-wishing people, couldn't we see them as manifestations of some deity that is trying to help us?

R: In the Tantric as well in the Mahayana sense, those who are trying to harm us are actually helping us. They help us to practice the paramitas so that we can attain enlightenment. That's why Shantideva says, "If there are no people who irritate you, then how can you perfect the paramita of patience? If there are no people to make you angry, how can you perfect the paramita of discipline? If there are no people or phenomena to distract your mind from the perfect samadhi, then how can you perfect the path of the paramita of discipline?" Therefore, all of these things are really manifestations of enlightenment.

Q: If you had one true experience of rigpa, would you ever be confused again?

R: Generally speaking, rigpa can be experienced in meditation. But that experience is not ultimate rigpa. It is not the fullness of rigpa. There are three stages one goes through: understanding, experience, and realization. Realization becomes a critical quality on the path, because realization is the fullness of the experience of rigpa. You have to go through the different stages of experiences and not get attached to them. Go continuously on the path. Eventually, that will lead to realization. When you have the realization of rigpa, that realization is irreversible.

Q: Is there a buildup of awareness that happens by the practice of recognizing or looking for your own basic nature so that, over time, it dispels the fear of these emotions?

R: Yes, awareness is developed through the discipline of meditation. Beginning with shamatha meditation, we develop lots of awareness and mindfulness on the path. Then, in Mahamudra and Dzogchen, we emphasize a different aspect of mindfulness and awareness. Mindfulness and awareness come from the discipline of meditation, which continues in our everyday life. Therefore, formal sitting practice is very important for us. For that reason, many teachers tell us to sit at least 10-15 minutes every day. That helps us to generate this continuity of awareness in our everyday life. There is no easy solution for manifesting awareness or mindfulness in our everyday life without some discipline in practice. The only problem is that when a student hears a teacher say that they must sit every day, that's the time students usually begin to change their guru!

Q: With respect to the fundamental ground, are rigpa, primordial purity, kadak, and lhündrup synonymous or are they different concepts?

R: In the most fundamental sense, they are all the same. Rigpa is kadak, kadak is rigpa. Kadak is also lhündrup, spontaneously-present wisdom, and that spontaneously-present wisdom is primordially pure. The unity of spontaneous presence and primordial purity is rigpa. In the sense of the ground, we can say they are the same. At the same time, there is also the Rigpa Kuntuzangpo, which is more of a resultant element. Rigpa can mean both.

PART FOUR

Experiencing Liberation

I, Samantabhadra,
Know naturally that ground
Without cause and condition.
I am without the defects of superimposition and denial
    of outer and inner.
I am unobscured by the darkness of mindlessness.
Therefore, self-appearance is unobscured.
If self-awareness remains in place,
There is no fear even if the threefold world is destroyed.
There is no attachment to the five desirables.
In self-arisen, nonconceptual awareness
There is no solid form or five poisons.

The unceasing lucidity of awareness
Is five wisdoms of one nature.
Through the ripening of the five wisdoms
The five families of the first buddha arose.
From the further expansion of wisdom
The forty-two buddhas arose.
As the display of five wisdoms
The sixty blood drinkers arose.
Therefore, ground-awareness never became confused.

As I am the first buddha,
Through my aspiration
May beings of saṃsāra's three realms
Recognize self-arisen awareness
And expand great wisdom.

My emanations are unceasing.
I manifest inconceivable billions,
Displayed as whatever tames beings.
Through my compassionate aspiration
May all beings of saṃsāra's three realms
Escape the six states.

◈| Spontaneous Awareness

THE NEXT SECTION OF THE PRAYER deals with how the buddha
Samantabhadra has experienced liberation.

> *I, Samantabhadra,*
> *Know naturally that ground*
> *Without cause and condition.*

It is pretty straightforward. Samantabhadra, the primordial buddha
himself, affirms that the ground is neither caused nor conditioned by
anything. It is beyond concept and beyond creation.

> *I am without the defects of superimposition and denial*
>   *of outer and inner.*
> *I am unobscured by the darkness of mindlessness.*
> *Therefore, self-appearance is unobscured.*

"I am" refers to Samantabhadra, Kuntuzangpo, the utterly pure
state of mind. It's free from the darkness of mindlessness. This means
that the state of Kuntuzangpo is a state of complete awareness. It is
complete mindfulness, primordially and always. For that reason, the
manifestations of Kuntuzangpo, which is our rigpa nature of mind,
are unobscured. The basic nature of self-appearances is free from any
obscuration of the conceptual mind of duality. When we experience

the self-appearing nature of phenomena, be they outer or inner, they are free from duality right from the beginning.

These appearances are self-manifestations. They manifest from the basic ground of rigpa and are the manifestations of rigpa. Those manifestations that you experience as forms, as outer and inner universes, are completely free from any stain. They are untainted by any defilements. They are completely pure in their own state.

The manifestations we experience as outside appearance are a simple manifestation of luminous mind. This luminosity, the clarity nature of our mind, gets to a point of intensity. When we don't recognize that intensity as the clarity nature of mind, it is projected outside and duality begins. When you recognize this intensity of luminosity as a self-manifestation, the appearances are not stained. They are completely pure in the state of kadak and lhündrup.

The ground is not tainted by the darkness of mindlessness. So, if we sustain this awareness, if we have the strength to be with this awareness, we can realize the nature of the ground. The nature of the ground is not polluted by mindlessness because it is fundamentally inseparable from awareness. Rigpa is not polluted by outside appearances. Therefore, its natural manifestation of appearances is not polluted. When we experience the world of naturally-arising appearances, we do not drift away from the fundamental ground of awareness that is rigpa. In the path of Dzogchen or Mahamudra, we relate with the day-to-day living experiences of the world and see them as in this nature of alpha-purity.

This state of undefiled awareness is realized only through mindfulness. Mindfulness is taught to be very important in the basic Mahayana path and plays a very important role in Dzogchen as well.

If self-awareness remains in place,
There is no fear even if the threefold world is destroyed.

This is my favorite line in Tibetan. If the self-awareness nature of mind rests in its nature of freshness, naked, without conceptualization or duality, then you are free from fear. There is nothing to fear, even if the threefold world is destroyed. In Buddhist cosmology, threefold world means countless worlds. So even if the planets that we live on and universes that exist around us get destroyed in front of you, your mind will remain in complete calm and peace without fear. If your mind can rest in the freshness of awareness like Kuntuzangpo, it will be completely at peace when you hear that a tornado has arrived.

One recognizes that nature and rests in it. One rests in the nature of primordial purity and spontaneously-existing wisdom. Resting means that there is continuity in the recognition. When recognition is continuous, that is called dwelling. If one is resting or dwelling in this basic state of ground, the pristine awareness that is the state of rigpa, then there is no fear. The recognition of the experience of rigpa cuts through any kind of fear. Even if the threefold world is coming to an end, rigpa is not shaken. It's a no-fear rigpa. Because it cuts through any root of confusion, through any root of illusion, the recognition of rigpa is emphasized here. That's the nature of Samantabhadra's recognition.

> *There is no attachment to the five desirables.*
> *In self-arisen, nonconceptual awareness*
> *There is no solid form or five poisons.*

"Attachment to the five desirables" refers to the five sensory pleasures and their objects, which are form, sound, smell, taste, and touch. Our basic attachment is to these five. If you really boil down our basic attachment to samsara, we are attached to these five desirable objects. We are attracted and attached to the beautiful forms of flowers, to the sounds of music, and so forth. When we realize the nature of the alpha-pure state of rigpa, we become free from the attachment to those five desirable objects.

There is no solid form of the five desirables and no solid form of the five poisons of passion, aggression, ignorance, jealousy, and pride. When passion arises, there's no solid form existing as passion. When aggression arises, there's no solid form of aggression, and so on. All of the poisons arise in the nature of self-arisen awareness. "Self-arisen" is similar to the notion of the connate or co-emergent nature of mind. When we talk about the self-arisen in the nondual sense, we're basically talking about a vivid experience of anything. Any vivid experience has this nature of self-arisen nondual experience. When you have that vividness, and awareness within that vividness, the experience is somehow beyond concepts of duality. That's the view of practice in Dzogchen and Mahamudra.

When you see these poisons arising, you see the self-arisen awareness. When you see the poisons manifesting so vividly, so nakedly, and so abruptly, you have a greater chance of awakening. When you don't have these vivid, abrupt, powerful, and overwhelming emotions, you have a lesser chance of awakening, according to the Mahamudra and Dzogchen view.

When these five desirable objects manifest in the paths of Dzogchen and Mahamudra meditation, they manifest so vividly. The experiences are so vivid and so close. It's not like talking about rigpa. It's not like talking about alayajnana. When you talk about alayajnana, rigpa, or ordinary mind, it sounds like some kind of theory. It sounds like something that we will experience in the future but don't see now. But, the experience of the five poisons and the five desirable objects is so vivid. From the Dzogchen point of view, they are so close. They are right in front of us. Therefore, there's a greater chance to experience your awakening mind through these experiences.

One can bring oneself to the experience of the ground by resting in the spontaneously-arising awareness, rather than being attached to the enjoyment of the five samsaric sensory objects. Not being attached to these appearances means that our discursive thought is not involved in solidifying these objects, in solidifying our perceptions, and in solidifying our concepts. We are then free from the five poisons of the mind, including the three basic poisons of desire, also known as attachment; hatred, also known as aggression; and delusion, also known as ignorance; as well as the poisons of pride and jealousy. One is free from these five poisons if one's sensory perceptions simply experience what they are without labeling thoughts.

This is very similar to Tilopa's instruction to Naropa. At the end of Naropa's trials and tribulations, Tilopa hit him on the forehead with his sandal and said, "You are not bound to samsara by appearances, you are bound to samsara by conceptual attachment. Therefore my son, Naropa, cut the root of this attachment." The appearances of the world outside, which are the experiences of the five sensory perceptions, are not a problem. The problem here is the labeling process that follows it.

Whatever sensory experiences we go through, if we go through them with mindfulness and awareness, there is no limit to how far we can go. The limit is mindfulness and awareness. Even if we don't enjoy the experience, that itself becomes a trip. The nonenjoyment becomes a cause of suffering. That's why, if we don't practice mindfulness and awareness, asceticism just becomes pain rather than a cause for liberation. That's why Buddha said to forget about asceticism. That's what Buddha did. He left asceticism, became very mindful in every step, and achieved enlightenment.

To develop mindfulness and awareness, it is important to practice stillness first. Theoretical aspects of the teachings are important for our studies, but just forget about all that when it comes to practice. Just sit and try to develop a certain fundamental power over your discursive thoughts as well as over your mind, to direct it wherever you want.

That is the purpose of our meditation here, to develop the power of our mind so that we can direct it wherever we want. We can direct our mind on a fountain pen and it can just be there. We can direct our mind on a statue of the Buddha and it just stays there. We can direct our mind to our breath and it just stays there. We're trying to develop that sense of pliancy of mind, which is important at this point. Neither alayavijnana or alayajnana matters at first, just get the stillness. In that stillness, the alayajnana arises naturally and without struggle. We don't need to say, "I want to focus my mind on alayajnana." When we are resting in that state, the jnana, the wisdom, manifests beautifully.

Jamgon Kongtrul the Great gave an example of this. If you stir water that is a little dirty in order to clean it, then it will become muddier. If you just let it sit, the dust will settle down and the water becomes clear. The clarity comes naturally. Alayajnana will come naturally in the process of settling alayavijnana.

Being mindful is the best discipline as well as the hardest one. Just shutting off sensory perceptions from objects is easy. If there is a visual joy, we can just turn our back on it. We can shut ourselves up in a mountain cave. But if we are not mindful, we carry the whole distraction into the cave. The causes of pain continue and the pain is still there. The discipline actually is mindfulness. It's not easy. If we practice that mindfulness discipline, then it doesn't really matter what sensory or conceptual experiences we are going through.

How to practice discipline is the question. Shantideva said that our mind is like a crazy wild elephant. It's like an elephant in a china shop. By just turning around, the elephant can destroy a tremendous number of things in the shop. The elephant is just making a simple innocent move. It is thinking, "I am just moving around." That's what we all think, don't we?

The first thing we need to do is to ground this elephant. This elephant is swimming in his crazy ideas, in his wildness, so we need to chain him down. That chain is mindfulness, which is the first step to actually bringing this crazy elephant down to earth. How do we accomplish that chaining? It is like staying in a house. In order to be protected, we need to lock our windows and our door. And if we are in New York City, we need three locks.

The purpose of locking our gate, our door, and our windows is so that our guests will not give us surprise visits. With that protection, the only possible way to enter our space is by ringing the doorbell. Whenever the doorbell rings, we go to our door. We look through the peephole and we have the opportunity, the space, to identify our guests. There is no surprise. We identify our guests, "Oh, my visitor is Mr. Anger" or "This time my visitor is Mr. Jealousy" or "This visitor is Mr. Ignorance." Then, with the great Mahayana compassion and the Vajrayana fearlessness, you open the door.

We won't leave our guest outside, we will invite him in. Be with it, that's the reality. In the house, we move with more awareness because the guest is there. We don't feel comfortable just doing anything we like. If we are respectful of the guest, we don't play loud music. As our guest is there, we don't walk naked in our room. Because of our guest, we are always aware. Therefore, we relate properly with the guest. Then, at the end, just let the guest leave at the time of its departure. We should not cling to this guest as a permanent member of the house because a guest is a temporary visitor. Don't hold on to it.

⚛ Five Wisdoms

THE NEXT SECTION OF THE PRAYER talks about the self-appearing spontaneous wisdom within which, in the case of Samantabhadra, full awakening is manifested. The absolute reality of rigpa, which is the true essence of wisdom, the true fundamental nature of phenomena, arises from this one nature. The spontaneous wisdom of kadak manifests within this one absolute reality.

> *The unceasing lucidity of awareness*
> *Is five wisdoms of one nature.*

When we look at the wisdom of kadak, its essence is shunyata, egolessness. It also has the quality of spontaneous luminosity, which is the primordial clarity that is basic lucidity. This wisdom manifests in the unceasing play of compassion.

"The unceasing lucidity of awareness" refers to these three aspects of the wisdom of kadak. In Dzogchen terms, these are called *ngowo*, *rangshin*, and *tukje*. *Ngowo* is "essence," *rangshin* is "nature," and *tukje* is "compassion." That's a complete understanding of the wisdom of kadak. Ngowo is emptiness, shunyata, egolessness, selflessness. Rangshin is lhündrup ösel, which is spontaneous clarity or basic lucidity. Tukje is the compassion of the kadak wisdom, which is the noble or genuine heart. It is the unceasing manifestation of pure love, pure compassion.

The wisdom of alpha-purity is fundamentally free from obscurations. It is the dharmata state, which is the dharmadhatu nature. Appearances freely manifest in that space of dharmadhatu, in the nature of mirrorlike appearances. No matter what appears, no matter in what aspect or in what different clarity it may appear, all appearances are in the same nature of that one wisdom. There's a sense of equality, of equanimity.

That state of wisdom is completely free from any aspect of delusion. In that nature of wisdom, it is free from any aspect of unclarity or fuzziness. It is free from fuzzy logic. The sense of freedom from unclarity is in the nature of total and complete discrimination. Such freedom does not rely on any effort in this fundamental state of wisdom. All actions arise spontaneously. They are accomplished effortlessly in this state of wisdom.

The wisdom of kadak is five wisdoms of one nature. That one nature is alpha-pure. It is the oneness of the three-kaya buddhahood, the oneness of the five-kaya buddhahood, and the oneness of the five wisdoms of the buddha. The one nature of the five wisdoms is described as the sun and the sunlight, or the moon and the moonlight. They are in one nature yet they are different.

The wisdom of buddhahood, the wisdom of enlightenment that is the fully matured aspect of rigpa, manifests as these five wisdoms. The five wisdoms are the dharmadhatu wisdom; the mirrorlike wisdom; the wisdom of equality; the wisdom of discriminating; and the wisdom of accomplishment.

Dharmadhatu wisdom is the basic state of being completely pure. *Dharma* is "phenomena." *Dhatu* is the "essence" or "truth," "the nature." So dharmadhatu means the true essence of phenomena. Dharmadhatu wisdom is the wisdom of seeing the true nature of phenomena. That true nature of phenomena has never been born. Phenomena, from the beginning, have never arisen as confusion. These confusions, the solidity of the phenomenal world, have never existed in the middle because they have never arisen. Because they have neither arisen in the beginning nor existed in the middle, there is no cessation of that confusion. It's pretty simple.

The emotional disturbances of samsaric phenomena have no cessation. There is no cessation of that ego-clinging. There is no cessation of our self-centricity. There is no end because it never existed to begin with. It has never been given birth to. The wisdom of seeing that true nature of phenomena is what we call dharmadhatu wisdom. This is the first wisdom of buddha.

The unimpeded nature of this clarity manifests like images in a mirror. That is the second wisdom, called "mirrorlike wisdom." The mirrorlike wisdom of buddha has the quality of egolessness because it is free from ego-identification. This wisdom is beyond conceptual seeing and beyond conceptual understanding. Therefore, it is taught with the example of a mirror.

If we place ourselves in front of a big mirror, everything appears instantaneously. It doesn't happen that first one row of images arises, then a second row, then a third row, and so on. At the same time, a mirror does not identify each thing that reflects in it. It does not say, "Okay, now the trees are reflecting. Now the carpet is reflecting. Now the people are reflecting. These are such and such people. This is such and such color of reflection." There is no such egotism in that wisdom nature. In a mirror, everything reflects simultaneously. Therefore, this is called "mirrorlike wisdom."

In a similar way, for a buddha, the phenomena of the three times reflect simultaneously. Everything arises simultaneously. There is neither a progression of seeing nor a progression of conceptualization. A buddha sees the three times in one instant. That is the example of mirrorlike wisdom.

As we discussed, in whatever variety they may appear, appearances are in the same nature. That's the third wisdom, called "the wisdom of equality or equanimity." This refers to the wisdom of selflessness.

Selflessness leads us to the ultimate realization of equanimity. Equanimity here refers to the equality of duality. It means there is no longer any difference between the self of phenomena and the self of person. The distinction of duality as perceiver and perceived is no longer made at this point.

Therefore, the wisdom of buddha sees the true nature of this equal state. Whether you are looking at the phenomenal world outside, such as a table, a house, mountains, and so forth, or at your own self as a person, they are equally selfless. Both rest in the same nature of equality that is emptiness, shunyata. The realization that is the ultimate seeing of that selfless nature is what we call the wisdom of equality.

The wisdom of equality arises in the bodhisattva path from the practice of exchanging oneself for others. We try to see the suffering of others, and we try to take the pain from others. We try to transcend our self-clinging through taking on the self-clinging of others. As a result, you get this wisdom called "the wisdom of equanimity."

The fourth wisdom is the wisdom of discrimination, which is completely free from delusion. It is a sense of sharpness and precision. Discriminating wisdom refers to a buddha's wisdom of seeing relative reality. Mirrorlike wisdom is the basic clarity that reflects in the mirror while discriminating wisdom sees the distinctive features and qualities individually. It is the wisdom of seeing appearances, of seeing how things exist. For example, it is the wisdom to discriminate the nature of the outer phenomena as being impermanent and the nature of phenomena as being emptiness. It is the wisdom to discriminate the nature of things existing in different levels of confusion in the samsaric realm. That wisdom is called "the wisdom of discrimination."

There is an example of how buddhas see this. If one of us falls asleep and has a nightmare, or has some painful illusion in a dream, a person with clairvoyance can see that. He can see that sleeping person going through tremendous pain for no reason. That person is experiencing a lot of fear in the dream. Maybe that person is being chased by a poisonous snake or a tiger. In that dream, he has objects of fear and he has a subject who fears. He is running through that illusion of pain.

For the person who is clairvoyant, none of this exists. The person who sees is not going through the suffering. He can see that the sleeping person is simply dreaming. The clairvoyant person knows that if this person awakens from the dream, then he will be totally free from that illusion of fear. So the clairvoyant person may try to wake this person up by using a particular method, perhaps by speaking a little bit louder. Such seeing by a clairvoyant person is what we call "the discriminating wisdom of a buddha."

All of these wisdoms arising naturally, spontaneously, and effortlessly is the fifth wisdom, called "the all-accomplishing wisdom." The all-accomplishing wisdom refers to the manifestations of a buddha's activities. This wisdom, manifesting in such outstanding ways, can be so beneficial to wake people up from the dream. The wisdom of knowing the best method to awaken beings from the nightmare of samsara is called "the all-accomplishing wisdom."

Accomplishing all the relative and ultimately-beneficial things for all sentient beings is what we call "all-accomplishing wisdom." Therefore, buddha sometimes uses the bucket of water method to wake someone up. If you use a bucket of water, sometimes the sleeping person might die from the shock, or perhaps have a heart attack. In those circumstances, buddha wouldn't use a bucket of water, but would instead simply present an alarm clock to this person. The different methods of accomplishing enlightenment are called "the all-accomplishing wisdom."

These are the five wisdoms in one, as it is taught. This explanation is not from my first-hand experience. It is from my first-hand conceptual understanding of the five wisdoms of a buddha.

◈| Buddha Families

THE PRAYER CONTINUES with the further manifestation of the five wisdoms of the alpha-pure nature:

Through the ripening of the five wisdoms
The five families of the first buddha arose.

In other words, from these five wisdoms we get the principles of the five buddha families. This doesn't necessarily mean five separate beings. We are talking about the five different elements of the wisdom of buddha, such as dharmadhatu wisdom and so forth. The five buddha families also arise from the five poisons of mind. According to Tantra, this is because the essence of our five poisons of mind is in the essence of the five buddha families. It is pretty amazing, pretty inconceivable.

When we look at these five wisdoms of a buddha, they are actually the nature of the five poisons. The essence of ignorance, the true nature of ignorance, exists in the nature of dharmadhatu wisdom. The wisdom of dharmadhatu is the absolute nature of the poison of ignorance. It exists, or arises, in the nature of Vairochana Buddha, the buddha in the center of the five buddha families. Vairochana is of that family called the Buddha family. Vairochana is the embodiment of the body essence of the buddhas. In the ordinary state, that wisdom is the nature of the skandha of form.

Mirrorlike wisdom is the absolute nature of the poison of aggression and hatred. That wisdom, as well as that poison, is in the nature of Akshobhya Buddha, the buddha of the eastern direction. Whenever aggression arises, it is the manifestation of Akshobhya. The mirrorlike wisdom manifests in the form of aggression when we are confused. Akshobhya Buddha belongs to the Vajra family and is the embodiment of the mind essence of the buddhas. In terms of the skandhas, it is the skandha of feeling.

In a similar way, the wisdom of equanimity is the absolute nature of the poison of pride. The transcendent nature of pride, that essence or fundamental state of pride, exists in the nature of Ratnasambhava. Ratnasambhava, the buddha of the southern direction, is in the nature of the wisdom of equality. Ratnasambhava Buddha is the manifestation arising from the transcendent nature of pride. The qualities of all the buddhas are embodied in one manifestation, Ratnasambhava. In terms of the skandhas, it is the skandha of perception and it belongs to the Ratna family, obviously.

The wisdom of discriminating awareness is the absolute nature of passion. The essence of our desire is in the nature of Amitabha Buddha, the buddha of the western direction. Amitabha Buddha manifests from the transcendent quality of passion. That nature of Amitabha Buddha manifests in discriminating wisdom. The manifestation of all the buddhas' speech is embodied in Amitabha. It is the skandha of formation, and belongs to the Padma family.

The all-accomplishing wisdom is the absolute nature of the poison of jealousy. It manifests in the northern direction and is called Amoghasiddhi Buddha. The all-accomplishing wisdom of buddha is the result of the transcendent nature of our poisonous emotion of jealousy. In the Vajrayana sense, the genuine essence of jealousy is the nature of Amoghasiddhi Buddha. Amoghasiddhi Buddha is the embodiment of all the activities of buddha. Therefore, this buddha family is called the Karma family. Karma means "action" or "activity." It is the skandha of consciousness.

When we look at this progression of how the wisdom of rigpa manifests in Tantra, we can clearly see that everything arises from rigpa. There is only one rigpa, one origin, one basis. It is the true nature of our mind. It manifests outside in these five different aspects in which everything is included. No matter what outer and inner appearances we experience, they all exist in the sphere of the five buddha family wisdoms that boil down to one essence. That condensed essence is rigpa.

The Dzogchen tantras are the basis of such presentations of the five buddha families. They are presented in detail in the teachings of the Dzogchen lineage, especially by Padmasambhava.

❧ Deity Principle

WHEN RIGPA MANIFESTS with the uncovered five wisdoms, which are the transcendental natures of our five poisons, it is like revealing the beautiful buddha in the vase. The covering vase has been broken. That transcendental nature is what we call the resultant stage of rigpa. The resultant stage not only manifests as primordial buddhas in the five buddha families, but,

> From the further expansion of wisdom
> The forty-two buddhas arose.
> As the display of the five wisdoms
> The sixty blood drinkers arose.

It's getting more exciting! When these wisdoms expand and manifest further, it is because of the compassion of the buddhas. The buddhas see the different needs of suffering sentient beings. It is very obvious, very easy, and very clear. According to the Dzogchen tantras, the buddhas manifest in different forms and in different realms to alleviate the different sufferings of all sentient beings.

Altogether, there are over one hundred different emanations of buddha that manifest. These are just one simple buddha called Kuntuzangpo manifested in a hundred different forms. There are not only five buddha families, but there are forty-two peaceful buddhas and

sixty wrathful buddhas. Usually it's fifty-eight wrathful manifestations, but here it is counted as sixty. We usually call the one hundred
manifestations *dampa rik gya*. This is similar to the practices of shitro,
the bardo teachings, where we talk about forty-two peaceful deities
and fifty-eight wrathful deities.

What are these forty-two and sixty buddhas? Briefly, with respect
to the forty-two peaceful manifestations, we have Kuntuzangpo Buddha and Kuntuzangmo, the female buddha, together. Then we have
the five buddhas of the five buddha families that we previously discussed. These are called the five male buddhas. Then we have five
female buddhas, called *ying chug ma*, who are their consorts. *Ying*
means "space," so they are called the "five female buddhas who have
power in space." Then we have eight male bodhisattvas, and eight
female bodhisattvas. According to Nyingma tradition, each realm has
its own buddha, so there are the six buddhas of the six realms. Finally,
we have four male gatekeepers and four female gatekeepers. That
makes forty-two peaceful emanations of buddha. If you are interested
in the details, these can be studied in the bardo teachings.

From the further manifestation of wisdom, the sixty wrathful manifestations of buddha arose. This is a very Vajrayana thing. If you're not
ready, just shut off your senses. You don't have to listen. The wrathful
manifestations are male and female wrathful herukas, wrathful buddhas, bodhisattvas, and other deities. They are known here as the sixty
blood drinkers.

The Tantric teachings are said to really benefit those who have very
strong poisons, very strong emotions. For that reason, the wrathful
deities play a stronger role on the path of awakening in Tantra. I think
that Tantric deities manifest with more extreme measures because of
the intensity of our poisons. Padmasambhava said that in the kaliyuga,
the polluted age, Tantra manifests in its full power and energy. From
the general Buddhist point of view, the polluted age is a very depress-

ing idea: things are getting worse and worse and worse. But from the Tantric point of view, it's not too bad. We have a greater opportunity to use the full power of Tantra.

The wrathful manifestations begin with heruka. Heruka is a more wrathful style of a buddha, a more yogic style. The heruka here is called Mahottara Heruka. The meaning of *mahottara* is "the most supreme."

Heruka and his consort are two. Then there are five male blood drinkers and five female blood drinkers. I like to use that phrase again and again. It sounds very yummy. Then there are eight yoginis, which are called the *gaurima gye*, and then the eight tramen goddesses. The tramen goddesses are depicted in the thangka paintings as having human bodies, but with different kinds of heads, such as the heads of different types of birds, and so on. Then you have four female gate-keepers, and the twenty-eight ishvaris. That's the sixty.

It says very clearly in the tantras and the teachings that however they may manifest, these forty-two and sixty deities are completely self-arisen and self-appearing. They are the appearance of different aspects of our own mind manifesting in these forms. They are not literal. They are very symbolic teachings. We must learn the meaning of each symbol before we do the practice of Tantra. When you have emanations of buddha in the forms of different Tantric deities, one must learn each detail in order to understand them fully. It is very important in Tantra to fully understand the details before we even try to recite the mantra or perform any rituals. We must go into those details before we try to conceptualize who or what the deities are.

Maybe these are not very important to you at this point. But if you read the *Tibetan Book of the Dead* in the future, it may be helpful. If you happen to be in the bardo, it may be helpful to at least know who the peaceful and wrathful deities are. Woody Allen said, "I don't believe in reincarnation but I will bring along a change of underwear anyway." So you might pack this extra underwear in case you need it.

Although we have these different manifestations of buddha in Tantra, it says very clearly,

Therefore, ground-awareness never became confused.

The fundamental nature of rigpa is naked awareness. That naked awareness, which is the ground luminosity, has never been polluted. The fundamental nature of mind has never been deluded. On that basis, and from that ground which is the naked pristine awareness of rigpa, all these buddhas and wisdoms of buddha manifest. It is the only source of these manifestations. It is the only reason why they manifest.

The ground-awareness refers to the wisdom of kadak. It refers to that one wisdom which appears in the five buddha families, which appears in one hundred deities, and so on. All of these boil down to one basic fundamental alpha-pure wisdom of kadak, which has never been confused in its own state. Its own state has always been awake and has always been fresh. It is free from any defilement. Therefore,

As I am the first buddha,
Through my aspiration
May beings of saṃsāra's three realms
Recognize self-arisen awareness
And expand great wisdom.

The aspiration we are making here is for all beings to recognize their self-arisen awareness, which arises in five wisdoms, in forty-two peaceful wisdoms, and in sixty wrathful wisdoms. These wisdoms are all self-arisen. We aspire that the self-arisen wisdom of the alpha-pure nature expands. We aspire that through the expansion of this wisdom, countless beings will benefit through countless different methods and countless different appearances of wisdom.

When we listen to a peaceful talk, it has probably been our experi-

ence that it doesn't always click our minds into the state of nonconceptual wisdom. It sort of goes through and . . . whoosh. It's almost
there, but it slips away. Or, you fall asleep at the very moment you're
supposed to get it. But at a certain point, some kind of very unpleas-
ant situation comes up that really gets us into that state. That unpleas-
ant situation really clicks us into the state of truly understanding and
appreciating impermanence. It clicks us into understanding shunyata
and appreciating the notion of emptiness. That happens all the time.

In a similar way, the wisdom of mind, which is the awakening heart,
does not always work with this peaceful manifestation. We slip away
all the time. Sometimes the wrathful manifestations of buddhas or
wisdoms really do the job. They really awaken some sentient beings.
Therefore, the peaceful and wrathful buddhas manifest for different
purposes.

As far as Dzogchen is concerned, we are in the nature of primordial
buddha. Because our nature of mind has never moved from that state
of primordial buddha, it has always been in the state of Kuntuzangpo.
It has always been in the state of enlightenment. Therefore, we are
making this aspiration with enlightened attitude and enlightened
desire.

We are not praying for sentient beings to achieve more samsaric
wealth, more samsaric joy, and more confusion. We are making the
aspiration that they obtain the ultimate wealth and the ultimate joy,
which is the recognition of primordial buddha mind. That is our aspiration here. But our aspiration is not only to recognize this primordial
ground of buddhahood. Once we have recognized this ground, we
aspire that such wisdom then expands and shines out. We aspire that
by recognizing this ground, the boundless wisdom of beings grows to
the infinite space of the universe.

There are many different aspirations we can make. We can make relative bodhicitta aspirations, saying, "May all sentient beings achieve
happiness, be free from suffering and the causes of suffering," and so

forth. But this aspiration of Samantabhadra is not for relative bod-hicitta, it is for ultimate bodhicitta. We are saying, "May all sentient beings, including ourselves, be in the state of our fundamental bud-dhahood that is the primordial buddha Samantabhadra." It is a very absolute aspiration, a very profound aspiration that we are making.

The next section talks about how Samantabhadra manifests in the appearances of other sentient beings as well as how Samantabhadra aspires to benefit other sentient beings through emanations.

> *My emanations are unceasing.*
> *I manifest inconceivable billions,*
> *Displayed as whatever tames beings.*
> *Through my compassionate aspiration*
> *May all beings of saṃsāra's three realms*
> *Escape the six states.*

If you want to do an aspiration to benefit others, this is a beautiful aspiration for all beings of the six realms.

As Guru Padmasambhava says about the manifestations of Karma-pas, "Until the end of sentient beings' confusion, the manifestations of enlightened Karmapa will not cease." It is also said that the mani-festations of Karmapa appear in a hundred million different universes. This means that enlightened teachers like Karmapa can manifest in different universes and on different planets as different masters.

The Second Karmapa said that during his lifetime, at that very moment, he had three emanations. One was somewhere else in central Tibet, another one was in China, and one was in eastern or western Tibet. It's a living example of so many things that are expressed in Samantabhadra's aspiration. At the same time, historically, there is only one manifestation that holds the name of Karmapa. During the time of the Second Karmapa, there was just one that manifested as Karmapa. The rest manifested under different names; maybe they were called Mr. Chow Yang in China, and Tashi in eastern Tibet or what have you.

This is the aspiration to manifest in inconceivable numbers in accordance with the different needs of sentient beings. It is the aspiration to display as whatever tames beings. It is in this manner that bodhisattvas manifest in different ways. It's not necessary to be born as a prince, like Shakyamuni Buddha. Buddhas manifest in accordance with the situation. They manifest in whatever way they can in order to tame the suffering of sentient beings. For example, it is said that the next buddha, Maitreya Buddha, will not be a prince. He will be born as a Brahmin.

Without moving from this fundamental state of alpha-purity, through the manifestations of spontaneous luminosity and the compassionate display of wisdom, Kuntuzangpo emanates unceasing manifestations that are inconceivable in number. This clearly shows that the emanations we spoke of, the five buddha families and the hundred different manifestations of buddha, are simply one very small part of Kuntuzangpo's activity as buddha. Kuntuzangpo says very clearly that he manifests in billions of universes as whatever serves the purpose of benefiting sentient beings. If a particular manifestation will release beings from their samsaric causes of confusion, then Kuntuzangpo will arise in that form.

In a similar way, we are making the aspiration that all sentient beings depart from the delusion and pain of the six realms. The psychological pain of all six realms can happen in this life. On this very earth, we can go through all the psychological disorders of mind. We experience pain, suffering, intensity. Therefore, we aspire that all beings be free from the pain and suffering of the six realms as well as the causes of that pain and suffering. We aspire that they may achieve the complete liberation from samsara. That is our aspiration here. It is a more relative aspiration than the earlier one.

Question: How can "I, Samantabhadra" be nondual?

Rinpoche: On one level, Samantabhadra is making the aspiration that all sentient beings experience the absolute reality where there's non-dual awareness. We're trying to experience that. The other level is that Samantabhadra is making these aspirations in a relative world, through relative bodhicitta, through compassion and love, and through words and wisdom.

We have a certain element of duality as soon as we start to open our mouths and say some words. As soon as we start to think in a concep-tual way, there is a duality. But duality in the beginning is not bad because we can't be totally nondual right from the beginning.

At the beginning, there has to be some sense of dualistic practice, such as compassion. When you practice compassion, it's very dualis-tic. You look at sentient beings that are suffering and then you prac-tice compassion. You apply your bodhicitta, the six paramitas, and so forth in order to benefit those sentient beings, as well as yourself, on the path. In that way, duality leads us to the nondual experience of awareness. That aspect of the path of duality causes us to eventually experience nondual awareness.

Q: Can you give some recommendations for postmeditation?

R: In the beginning, you should put some effort into your postmedi-tation practice. For example, you should try to remember to watch your mind, watch your thoughts, at least once every hour. That's very good practice already. If you do it every hour, it is already a great achievement. Later, that effort will bring the sense of effortless aware-ness in everyday life.

I use a digital watch. If you set it to beep every hour, you can tell yourself, "OK, when it beeps I will just look at my thought, once." You don't have to do anything more or less. Don't worry about sitting posture or anything, just look at your thought. Whenever it beeps, just look at your thought that very moment. Then you say, "Oh, aggression." Or maybe there was a positive thought, whatever. You may say that you are going to be mindful twenty-four hours a day, but that's not possible. But if you say, "I am going to be mindful every time my watch beeps," that's very possible. So every time it beeps, just look at your mind. See what emotions you are going through. Continue to just observe it as much as you can, as often as you can. If you forget, then your watch will remind you again.

You can use other methods as well. If you are driving a lot, then every time someone honks at you, you can watch your mind instead of shouting. I found that to be a nice method. It is certain that you will get angry when someone honks at you. If you watch your mind, you can see your anger coming up. You observe it. In that way, it becomes much easier and simpler to deal with. There are many different methods in life you can use. You can just set up whatever reminders are relevant to your life. Such practices lead us to continuous awareness.

At first, for bewildered beings
Awareness did not arise on the ground.
That obscurity of unconsciousness
Is the cause of bewildered ignorance.
From that unconsciousness
Emerged terrified, blurry cognition.
Self-other and enmity were born from that.
Through the gradual intensification of habit
Sequential entry into saṃsāra began.
The five poisonous kleśas developed.
The actions of the five poisons are unceasing.
Therefore, since the ground of the confusion of beings
Is mindless ignorance,
Through the aspiration of myself, the buddha,
May all recognize awareness.

The connate ignorance
Is a distracted, mindless cognition.
The labeling ignorance
Is holding self and other to be two.
The two ignorances, connate and labeling,
Are the ground of the confusion of all beings.
Through the aspiration of myself, the buddha,

May the thick, mindless obscurity
Of all samsaric beings be dispelled.
May dualistic cognition be clarified.
May awareness be recognized.

❧ Bewildered Ignorance

THIS SECTION SHOWS how samsara came to exist from the point of view of Dzogchen. It deals with the primary cause of samsara and how the other aspects of ignorance, delusion, or confusion arise from that.

> *At first, for bewildered beings*
> *Awareness did not arise on the ground.*
> *That obscurity of unconsciousness*
> *Is the cause of bewildered ignorance.*

The Dzogchen view is that deluded beings arise because of the failure to see the awareness of the original ground. The awareness, which did not arise on the ground, is the awareness of spontaneous insight, vipashyana, superior insight. This does not mean that rigpa is absent in the beginning. It is very much present. However, when we fail to recognize it, when it fails to recognize itself, the illusion begins. The whole of samsara manifests from that very moment of nonrecognition. In a way, it is very simple.

We search so much for the beginning of samsara. However, Buddha said many times that it is useless to search history to find it. He said that there was not much benefit in knowing. Knowing when or how samsara started is not going to really help us to undo it. Therefore, Buddha concentrated mainly on the path that can undo it, rather than going into the history and so forth.

It's like the big-bang theory. Scientists spent years and years and years finding out how the universe started. The only theory they came up with is just a big bang. That doesn't really help us much. Even scientifically, it doesn't help much. A big bang is a big bang.

Logically speaking, the answer is to look at this very moment: samsara begins right here. We don't have to trace back a hundred years, a thousand years, or a hundred eons. We can trace back the beginning of samsara to this very moment. From the Tantric, Mahamudra, and Dzogchen points of view, it is the beginning of our samsara and it could be the end of our samsara. At this very moment, the basic state of mind is intrinsically pure in that state of great clarity. However, we're not seeing it. Instead, there is the continuous pattern of ignorance and the other delusions that we have discussed.

For whatever reason, it is arising right now. There is really no long way to go back to find the beginning of this ignorance that arises on the basis of awareness. The text clearly says that not being mindful is what actually covers our awareness. Unmindfulness clouds our perception. In that state, we lose this basic luminosity. When we are in the state of mindlessness, we lose this basic awareness. The failure to recognize this ground awareness is the beginning of samsara, which is the situation of unawareness. Logically speaking, that is why the beginning of samsara is right here.

In Tibetan, it says *rigpa rang tsuk ma thuppa rigpa*, "rigpa has its own characteristics." When we fail to recognize and rest in that original state, when rigpa is not resting in its own characteristics, the delusions begin.

The basic ignorance here is not a conceptual ignorance. It is described as a state of unconsciousness. The obscurity of unconsciousness arises when the ground is not completely manifest. It is a state that lacks awareness. Losing our mindfulness is itself unawareness.

That unawareness, which we call ignorance, is the beginning. It's that simple. There is no awareness, no rigpa, when you're totally unconscious. When there is no rigpa, the ground that is in the state of primordial alaya does not manifest. That ignorance becomes the cause of all our samsaric delusions. Therefore, it is the root of samsara. For that reason, the Prayer says that the cause of bewildered ignorance is this basic unconsciousness.

In that state of basic unconsciousness, nothing is clear. In that state, not even duality manifests. It is a very heavy state of mind. It is a deep state of dullness, like torpor. In Tibetan, we have a saying to call someone *thom kyer*, which means "completely spaced out," "completely blank," "just sitting there." It is much worse than couch potatoes. That same word is used here. In that state of unconsciousness that has no awareness, even the clarity of duality is lacking. It completely lacks vividness. According to Dzogchen, this is the cause and beginning of samsara.

> *From that unconsciousness*
> *Emerged terrified, blurry cognition.*
> *Self-other and enmity were born from that.*

Now we can see that duality is coming. You know, good old duality is not that old. From the basic state of unclarity, that sense of totally lacking vividness, arises a second phase of confusion. This second phase is a terrifying experience. From that state of ignorance, conceptions start to arise in a kind of terror. Then we project some things as self and some things as other. From that beginning, we start to develop duality.

There is some sense of fear arising at this point because you are not very clear about the experience of clarity. The experience of the vivid world is arising, but you're not sure of your relationship with it. In a way, you can see that terror in the faces of babies when they're just born.

There is a sense of terror that arises when you come out of unconsciousness. Sometimes we have that experience when we take a siesta, at least I have. It's a very weird experience to wake up from a long siesta in the afternoon. It is a kind of terror. You don't know exactly what time it is. You think it's morning, but, when you look, the sun is just setting or it is already dark. It is like going from that unconscious state to consciousness. There is always a mysterious experience in that very moment of switch. We're not talking about a continuous experience of five or ten minutes, that's different. But in the very moment of waking up, you can feel that terror. There is some sense of fear, a sense of loss in direction, in time, in reference point, in everything.

So, this experience is nothing new. It seems to be something that we have experienced from the beginning of samsara. That's how the process takes place. When we first wake up, there's a blurry cognition, especially for those of us that need glasses! There's no doubt about it: the first thing we do is grab our glasses.

The experience of the terror, or the blurriness, comes from our mind failing to take its own place. It is our mind lacking the strength, so to speak, to remain in its own state of primordial buddhahood. There is a sense of weakness in that very particular experience. From there, we start our duality. The notion of self arises and, from that notion of self, the notion of other arises. From these two, we get caught up in the notions of enmity, friendship, and so forth. Then the good old samsaric game of duality begins to arise.

Dualistic mind develops first from the dominating ignorance. This dominating ignorance is the fundamental ignorance that we have been speaking about. It is the basic ignorance that we miss right at the beginning of every moment. I am not talking about a long time ago. I am talking about the beginning of any moment. We live in this illusion, thinking that fundamental ignorance is not there. We are meditating. We are mindful. Nonetheless, it is still there. It's existent and it's slippery. It is so slippery that we don't even recognize it.

✠| Five Poisons

Through the gradual intensification of habit
Sequential entry into saṃsāra began.
The five poisonous kleśas developed.
The actions of the five poisons are unceasing.

G RADUALLY WE INTENSIFY, gradually we solidify, and gradually we develop deeper impressions of this pattern of duality. This pattern repeats over and over and over. It becomes so solid and appears so genuine that it almost becomes part of us. It almost becomes the nature of our mind.

Whenever we think of mind, we are thinking about "I." That's duality. In gradual steps, we get deeper and deeper into this samsaric pattern. From that fundamental ignorance and the development of the split of duality, the actions of the five poisons increase. This develops into a stream of endlessly repetitive actions of the five poisons. We get into that mechanism of habitual pattern. Then we enter into samsara in a deeper sense, no matter what level of samsara we may be experiencing.

Once we have developed that degree of intensification or habituation, the mechanism doesn't stop. It continues to run automatically. The example we use in Buddhism is a potter's wheel. Some kind of effort is required for the potter to start turning the wheel. Once the wheel is turning, it doesn't stop. It just keeps going on and on and on, continuously. You actually have a hard time stopping it. Similarly, once we have turned the wheel of the five poisons, it doesn't stop. It's unceasing. Do you remember any break from the five poisons? It's very difficult. I don't quite remember having any break from the five poisons.

From this endless stream that we call karma, the samsaric solidity of suffering, of ego-clinging, and of poisonous emotions gradually develops. When that has developed, we end up in this solid existence of samsara. The progression that ends up as the existence of samsara is basically the twelve nidanas, the twelve links of interdependent origination. Beginning with ignorance, formation, and so forth, we have the inner cycle of twelve interdependent nidanas. We also have these twelve links in the outer sense: the twelve astrological cycles called the twelve months, the cycle of twelve years, and so on. From the repetition of the twelve interdependent originations, we solidify our habitual inclinations and tendencies. In that way, we solidify our samsara.

We have the habitual tendency to delude our perception. We delude our conception, our view, and our understanding. As a result of habitual tendencies, we are always caught up in this cyclic existence called samsara. We get caught in the continual cycle of the five poisons. The unbroken continuity of habitual tendency, the unbroken continuity of the five poisons, is the existence of samsara. It is the only reason we are bound to this suffering. It is the only reason we are caught up in this suffering. We learn here that samsara is nothing apart from our habitual delusion.

According to Dzogchen, the five poisons are nothing but the manifestation of the luminosity of rigpa. They are called *ö nga*, the five luminous lights. The five luminous lights of rigpa are white, yellow, red, green, and, like the color of Kuntuzangpo, deep blue.

Each of the five lights has meaning. The luminous white light of wisdom is the manifestation of rigpa's immaculate nature. That completely pure nature, that completely pacified nature, manifests as the white luminous light.

The yellow luminous light is the manifestation of rigpa's fully completed qualities. This means that rigpa is fully enriched with all the qualities of buddha. Rigpa is fully equipped, so to speak, with all the enlightened wisdoms necessary to overcome our emotions and ego-clinging. That completeness of qualities manifests as yellow light, which is richness.

The red luminous light is the manifestation of the quality of rigpa that encompasses and magnetizes. Like a magnet, it draws all things in that direction. In a similar way, that very nature of our mind called rigpa encompasses all qualities, encompasses all wisdom. This means that everything is included within rigpa, nothing is left outside. That's why we have this magnetizing red light, which encompasses all the qualities.

The difference between the yellow and the red light is that the yellow light of enriching has the quality of possessing all the many different elements of buddha wisdom, while the red light of magnetizing encompasses all these qualities that actually boil down to rigpa. It's rigpa that has all these qualities. So everything boils down to one and only one essence. The single essence, which that contains all, is rigpa. It is the primordial mind, the primordial wisdom.

The luminous green light means that rigpa manifests all the activities of buddha. Rigpa has the compassion, love, and wisdom that buddhas manifest as physical activity, verbal activity, and samadhi, meditative absorption. All of these activities of buddha are complete within rigpa. Symbolizing that is the luminous green appearance of light, which is the fourth light taught in Dzogchen.

The fifth light is the deep luminous blue light that symbolizes the unchanging nature of rigpa. No matter what confusions we may experience at this point, the true state of rigpa is beyond all confusion. No confusion, ego-clinging, or mind poison can ever touch the true state of rigpa. They can never cause it to change. The absolute state of our mind is in the unchanging nature of rigpa, the unchanging nature of the buddha wisdom. Therefore, we have this luminous blue light.

The five elements manifest from these five lights. The water element manifests from white light. The earth element manifests from yellow light. The fire element manifests from red light. The wind element manifests from green light, and the space element manifests from blue light. These are the five elements.

From these five lights, the five objects of the five poisons also manifest. When we fail to recognize the five-colored luminosity of rigpa manifesting, we misperceive it. We misperceive the luminous white light of rigpa as ignorance. We misperceive the luminous yellow light as pride. We misperceive the luminous red light as passion, desire, and attachment. We misperceive the luminous green light as jealousy, and we misperceive the luminous blue light as aggression. We misperceive these five luminous lights as the five poisons.

According to Dzogchen teachings, the five luminous lights can be the objects of the five poisons as well as the five poisons themselves. If you take them as the objects of the five poisons, then they correspond with the emotions as we have said. As the subjects of the five poisons, they are the five buddha families. Within the five buddha families, ignorance is Vairochana; aggression is Akshobhya; pride is Ratnasambhava; passion is Amitabha; and jealousy is Amoghasiddhi.

Since they do exist in that nature, the Prayer says that samsara begins as a result of the failure to recognize the true nature of the five poisons and their objects. Whenever these appearances of lights arise, these appearances of the five poisons, we can recognize them in their true nature as the five buddha families. We can recognize them in the nature of the five buddha wisdoms. If we recognize them, it becomes liberation. Therefore, Samantabhadra makes this aspiration, saying,

Therefore, since the ground of the confusion of beings
Is mindless ignorance,
Through the aspiration of myself, the buddha,
May all recognize awareness.

We have these five emotions within the five wisdoms. This is taught in Vajrayana Buddhism in general and Dzogchen in particular. Whenever we have ignorance, it is in the nature of dharmadhatu wisdom. When we have aggression or irritation, that exists in the nature of mirrorlike wisdom. When we have pride, that nature of mind exists in the wisdom of equanimity. When we have passion, desire, or attachment, that mind exists in the nature of discriminating wisdom. When we have jealousy or envy, it exists in the nature of all-accomplishing wisdom. Therefore, these five poisons remain in the five wisdoms of buddha.

It is important to identify the emotion in which we are engaged, even though it is often mixed. Passion, aggression, jealousy, and so on are all mixed at certain points. Identifying them is the process that naturally takes us to mindfulness, to awareness. There is no other way.

When we recognize an emotion, such as strong passion accompanied by jealousy, we are actually breaking down the speed of that emotion. The total sense of recognition is quite important in both Sutra and Tantra. In Sutra, it is mindfulness. In Tantra, if we see that nature and look at it nakedly, we will see the nature of that wisdom. You don't need to logically apply any reasoning. You don't need to conceptually meditate on anything. Just simply recognize and observe it. Whether it is dharmadhatu wisdom, mirrorlike wisdom, or any of the other five wisdoms, you will see the nature of that wisdom. We will have the experience of that wisdom by simply being with it without conception. Therefore, recognition is quite important.

The first step is just simply to observe it. Simply recognize the emotion and then watch it as it grows or as it continues. Just simply watch it. In the beginning, just to have an idea that it's coming is very important and very effective. In the Vajrayana sense, the way to watch these emotions is without stopping them. If we recognize the emotion and say, "Yes, it is passion," and then try to stop it, that's a problem. Rejecting our emotions is a problem in Vajrayana.

Instead of trying to stop it, let it come. Invite it more. Look at the nature of passion more nakedly. Look at the nature of aggression, look at the nature of ignorance, look at the nature of anything. Once we have received the pointing-out instruction from our vajra master, we know how to watch it. We know how to look at it. We don't have to leave something behind and go to a certain place called "liberation." That simple process of looking at it in every moment actually brings liberation on the spot. Within that nature of passion is liberation, within that nature of aggression is liberation.

If we know how to watch in that state, then we find the liberation within that passion. In the shamatha-vipashyana of Mahamudra practice, there are the shamatha methods of calming the emotions and the vipashyana methods of watching our emotions. In the Dzogchen tradition, there are the methods of Trekchö to cut through the emotions and the methods of Thögal to experience the luminosity of the emotion, of those states of mind. These things are details that we need to have pointed out.

Therefore, we're making the aspiration for all beings to recognize their awareness because awareness is the primary nature of our minds. Lacking the recognition of awareness, we get into the delusion of ignorance and the whole wheel of samsara. This is the view of Dzogchen. It's simple, right?

When we make this aspiration prayer of Samantabhadra, we do so remembering the nature of our five poisons. We do so remembering the samsaric chain in which we are caught and the process of samsaric existence. We do so remembering the true nature of rigpa, the five wisdoms, and the five families of Buddha Samantabhadra. We make this aspiration saying,

May all recognize their own radiant awareness.

Samantabhadra makes this prayer in order that all beings be free from the delusion of samsara and from the cause of that delusion. The cause of that delusion is unawareness, unmindfulness. Our aspiration is that all sentient beings recognize this true nature that we are beginning to discover, that we are beginning to familiarize ourselves with. May they be free from unmindfulness and achieve the wisdom to recognize their own radiant awareness.

⊰⊱| Ground of Confusion

FROM THE BASIC IGNORANCE that we discussed earlier, we fall into connate, or co-emergent, ignorance.

> *The connate ignorance*
> *Is a distracted, mindless cognition.*

"Connate" is a better term than "co-emergent." "Co-emergent" has the sense of two separate things merging into one, like two threads woven together. "Connate" is more accurate because it's one nature arising simultaneously. From that connate ignorance, the ignorance of false imagination is developed, which is known as *kundak*. Kundak is the ignorance of imputation. These are very helpful definitions of connate ignorance and of the labeling ignorance of false imagination. From these three ignorances, the dominating ignorance, the connate ignorance, and the ignorance of false imagination, we get more and more into the solid gross reality of duality.

Samantabhadra says that connate ignorance is unconscious, unmindful. It is unawareness. The dominating ignorance brings the connate ignorance, which arises simultaneously with our mind. The connate ignorance is together with every moment of our consciousness, with every moment of our awareness. We know it's there, but, each moment, we fail to recognize it. Right now we are saying to ourselves that we must recognize it, but the next moment we miss it again. And the next moment we say that to ourselves again. And then, the next moment, we miss it again. This repetitive failure to recognize the dominating ignorance is the connate ignorance.

The connate ignorance is actually the nature of not recognizing. At the very moment of not being aware, as one's consciousness is totally ignorant, pristine awareness is very much present. At the very moment I have a tremendous sense of emotion, it exists within the basic state of rigpa, the pristine awareness. This is what we call connate. In that very moment of experiencing ignorance, it is already in the nature of alpha-pure wisdom. It's not really arising at the same time; the alpha-pure wisdom is its basic nature. The nature of ignorance is the same as the nature of wisdom. It's always there. This nature of ignorance is the unawareness.

Every moment of consciousness arises together with that dominating ignorance. Ignorance and awareness are together at this point. If awareness were not present when the ignorance is present, then the awareness would not be the fundamental nature of mind. According to the text, these two are simultaneous at this point. So, awareness and ignorance are the two elements we are talking about as being co-emergent. They are awareness, rigpa, and ignorance, ma rigpa.

Connate ignorance is not the ordinary notion of distraction. It is not hearing a sound and then getting distracted to it, or seeing an image and getting distracted to that. We're not talking about a cause of distraction here. We are talking about a very subtle distraction from basic awareness. That distraction is described as mindless cognition. Just being mindless itself is a distraction. That's the most subtle distraction we ever experience in our meditation path.

Usually, we think of distraction as being something very active. We think of it as a dualistic interaction between an outside object and one of the six sensory perceptions. But distraction here is simply being unmindful, being unaware. This distraction refers to the basic sense of unconsciousness that we discussed earlier. This connate ignorance is not conceptual mind. It is the fundamental ignorance.

According to Tantra, that very co-emergence is unborn. It is non-existent. It is in the nature of rigpa. It is completely pure in the nature of kadak. From rigpa's point of view, there is no such connate ignorance. From the point of view of sentient beings, we have this inborn or connate ignorance when we don't recognize rigpa.

The labeling ignorance
Is holding self and other to be two.

Because of the connate ignorance, we develop the ignorance of false imagination. The ignorance of false imagination, which is sometimes called the ignorance of imputations, experiences the display of one's own manifestation of rigpa as something other than rigpa itself. We see the manifestation as other and interact with it in that way. At this point, we are beginning to go through the process of labeling, the process of conceptualization, and the process of imagination.

For example, we sometimes label the appearance of luminosity in our mind as enemy, sometimes as friend. Actually, we are simply experiencing our own imagination. What we see in our mind is not the person we are thinking about; it's our concept, our own thought. So the enemy is right within us. There is nothing outside. It is within us at the most basic level. At the level of rigpa, that very concept of enemy is the luminosity element of mind. The luminosity is misconceived as some outer element, as an enemy somewhere outside.

The co-emergent ignorance is the basis for the labeling and for imputations. It's like the canvas on which we paint different images. We must first have the canvas in order to create any image, in order to project or paint any of our creativity. The labeling ignorance is like the basic painting itself. We always talk about the co-emergent and labeling ignorances in Madhyamaka logic and in buddha nature theories. It is common to the Cittamatrin, the Madhyamaka, and the Vajrayana view.

The labeling process is very subtle. Even though we are characterizing the ignorance of false imagination as one process, it has many different layers. We usually have so many labeling processes going on, so many chains of thoughts. We say, "Passion is good, we should have passion." That labeling processes is not very enlightening. It's not emotion itself. It's not thought itself. We are grouping all these labeling processes as one at this point. The labeling process is a very subtle way of planting and growing this seed of ignorance in our mindstream.

This ignorance is connected to the five luminous lights that we misperceive as objects. Therefore, this ignorance is called the false imagination. As it says here, the most gross element of this ignorance is the division between self and other. The labeling process has matured to the stage where we can clearly see the dualistic barrier. That is the final stage of this ignorance.

> *The two ignorances, connate and labeling,*
> *Are the ground of the confusion of all beings.*

Because of these, we get involved in passion, aggression, and ignorance. As a result of those actions, we fall further into ignorance. Every illusion of samsara arises from this simple duality. Whether it's suffering, pain, or happiness, everything arises from ignorance. The Prayer says that the connate and labeling ignorances are the ground of the confusion of all beings. They are the bases, the fundamental causes of all samsaric illusions.

These three ignorances, the dominating ignorance, the connate ignorance, and the ignorance of false imagination, are accompanied by four conditions. First, there is the causal condition. The causal condition is not recognizing the manifestation of ground. It is not recognizing that the manifestations arise from the basic ground of luminosity, the basic ground of rigpa, the basic ground of the naked nature of our mind.

The second condition is called the objective condition. It is this condition through which these delusions arise. When the manifestations of rigpa arise as luminous, we confuse them as objects of samsaric perception, of ignorant perception. That is the objective condition.

The third condition is called the dominating condition. The dominating condition is our ego-clinging. Good old ego-clinging becomes the basic dominating factor, the dominating condition.

The fourth condition is called the instantaneous or immediate condition. It refers to the co-emergent nature of these three conditions together. The causal condition, the objective condition, and the dominating condition arising together is called the instantaneous or immediate condition. When the three ignorances and the four conditions come together, then we get the illusion of samsara.

The aspiration at this point is very beautiful:

> *Through the aspiration of myself, the buddha,*
> *May the thick, mindless obscurity*
> *Of all samsaric beings be dispelled.*
> *May dualistic cognition be clarified.*
> *May awareness be recognized.*

There is an expression in English, "thick-skulled." Samsaric beings are sometimes like that. They are thick-skulled. "All samsaric beings" includes ourselves. We don't have any openness to the idea of nirvana or liberation. We don't get enlightenment because we don't really want it.

According to Buddhist teachings, the resistance is coming from clinging on to our ego. Ego, our very old friend, has been so close to us for millions of years. We have shared our space with this old friend so much that at this point we have totally lost our sense of true existence, true nature. We have misidentified ourselves with this ego.

It is not an easy decision to kick this friend out of our room, out of our space, right now. On one hand, part of our mind is saying, "I really want to kick this friend out because it has been causing me a lot of pain." On the other hand, we are still attached to it because it is so close that it has almost become ourself.

The root of our problem of not being willing to achieve enlightenment is this: we can't let go of our ego-clinging. The way to overcome this is to see that ego has never given us any positive results. If we can see that, then we can develop more renunciation of ego and more renunciation of samsara. Then we can really kick this friend out from our space.

On the spiritual path, we see the possibility of freedom. We see the possibility of finally getting a sense of liberation from these irritating habitual tendencies. They are not fun anymore. Maybe it's fun to go to McDonald's once or twice. The third time is not really fun, but we are habituated, so we go back. We are disgusted with this.

There is no easy way. If anyone says it's easy and that we don't need diligence, it's not true. Everything needs a certain element of diligence, of exertion. With diligence and exertion, we can reach a point where effort becomes effortless. However, at the beginning we need to exert ourselves. In order to exert ourselves, we need discipline. That's why the paramita practices are so practical. The paramita practices are common to both Tantra and Sutra. We can begin with discipline, which is the cause of diligence, and discipline enforces our diligence. Diligence doesn't come without renunciation and without seeing the possibility of freedom. Therefore, they are all connected.

So making this aspiration and saying, "May the thick, mindless obscurity of all samsaric beings be dispelled" is very beautiful. When we make such an aspiration, it is important to first reflect on the nature of the three ignorances. We reflect on the nature of rigpa as well as its manifestation, and then we make these very simple aspirations of Samantabhadra.

Question: Is the difference between the dominant and the co-emergent ignorance a difference in time?

Rinpoche: The dominant ignorance is at the beginning. It is no wonder that it is difficult to see because it happens pretty early. When it's first arising, one does not see that arisal. The co-emergent ignorance arises in every moment of awareness. It is more like the continuity of that dominant ignorance. On the one hand, they're very similar: they are all in the same nature of ignorance. It is like when we talk about the five wisdoms of the buddha. On the one hand, you cannot separate them as they are all similar. On the other hand, they have slightly different qualities.

Q: Which comes first, karma or ignorance?

R: The dominant ignorance leads to the karmic cycle. Because of this ignorance, you have karma. Because of karma, your ignorance gets stronger. It covers the rigpa more. The sequence begins with ignorance in Tantra as well as in Sutra. For example, the twelve nidanas begin with ignorance. Because of ignorance, we commit wrong actions such as harming oneself or others. Therefore, ignorance comes first in the sequence.

Because we have gone through the cycle of the twelve nidanas so many times, often we feel that it comes from karma. Because of this, we have further ignorance and go around the loop again. So the cycle begins with ignorance, which can be intensified further with negative karma.

Q: You said that ego was a bad friend, but isn't the kind of friendship we make with our emotions really the question?

R: Of course, it is fine to have different understandings and different views. However, I don't think we need jealousy, for example, to obtain wisdom. Jealousy is one of the very difficult emotions to overcome. It can be very destructive. At the same time, we need to have a certain element of emotion to go beyond emotions. Therefore, at the beginning, we do not completely deny the emotions.

That's why bodhisattvas do not relinquish one element of desire. They need it to come back to samsara in order to benefit sentient beings. Therefore, they keep a certain element of passion, which is transformed by compassion. So, there are certain elements of emotions that are needed, but not really jealousy.

Perhaps you are talking about ambition rather than jealousy, like saying, "I want to be like Shakyamuni Buddha and the previous buddhas," or, "I want to be enlightened like all the other enlightened beings." In the beginning, that kind of ambition is very important. It's not bad. It is transcended later on the path. Maybe jealousy is helpful in some ways. Perhaps you work harder, you become more diligent on the path, because your colleagues are improving faster. In that sense, maybe jealousy is beneficial sometimes.

Let me speak a little about the relationship with ignorance. The basic view is that ignorance has always been a problem, ego has always been a problem. That's why we look at ego as the cause of suffering in the basic sense. As we have been discussing, ignorance is in the nature of Vairochana Buddha. The relationship changes: ignorance is not really bad at that point. The nature of ignorance is in Vairochana Buddha. The nature of that ignorance is dharmadhatu wisdom. The nature of that ignorance is the embodiment of the buddha's body. Different levels of the Buddhist path have different approaches to that relationship. Therefore, we may say that the relationship changes. The most fundamental view of Buddhism is that it is important for us to develop the desire for enlightenment at the beginning.

When anyone speaks about dharma, he is simply reflecting his view, his opinion, his understanding. So, when I talk about the Samantabhadra prayer, I'm speaking from my understanding, my training, my practice, and my experience. This is what I feel, what I think. This is very important for us to understand. It's the same with every subject.

The absolute thing is something that we should realize. It is something that we have to taste, to experience, and then say, "Ah, this is it." I think it is important for us not to take any speaker's view as an absolute authority. There is no such absolute authority. If you take any speaker as an absolute authority, then that would be Shakyamuni Buddha. It would be Buddha's speech, his teachings. So we may, to a certain degree, take anything that Buddha taught in the Buddhist canon as absolute authority. Other than that, we always say, "This is Nagarjuna's view" or "This is Asanga's view." That's very important.

Part Six

Dualism

Dualism is doubt.
From the emergence of subtle clinging
Coarse habit gradually develops.
Food, wealth, clothing, places, companions,
The five desirables, and beloved relatives—
Beings are tormented by attachment to the pleasant.
That is mundane confusion.
There is no end to the actions of dualism.
When the fruit of clinging ripens,
Born as pretas tormented by craving—
How sad is their hunger and thirst.
Through the aspiration of myself, the buddha,
May desirous beings
Not reject the longing of desire
Nor accept the clinging of attachment.
By relaxing cognition as it is
May their awareness take its seat.
May they attain the wisdom of discrimination.

Through the emergence of a subtle, fearful cognition
Of externally-apparent objects
The habit of aversion grows.
Coarse enmity, beating, and killing are born.

When the fruit of aversion ripens,
How much suffering there is in hell through boiling and burning.
Through the aspiration of myself, the buddha,
When strong aversion arises
In all beings of the six states,
May it be relaxed without rejection or acceptance.
Awareness taking its seat,
May beings attain the wisdom of clarity.

One's mind becoming inflated,
An attitude of superiority to others,
Fierce pride, is born.
One experiences the suffering of disputation.
When the fruit of that action ripens,
One is born as a god and experiences death and downfall.
Through the aspiration of myself, the buddha,
May beings with inflated minds
Relax cognition as it is.
Awareness taking its seat,
May they realize equality.

Through the habit of developed dualism,
From the agony of praising oneself and denigrating others,
Quarrelsome competitiveness develops.
Born as an asura, killed and mutilated,
One falls to hell as a result.
Through the aspiration of myself, the buddha,
May those who quarrel through competitiveness
Relax their enmity.
Awareness taking its seat,
May they attain the wisdom of unimpeded activity.

Through the distraction of mindless apathy,
Through torpor, obscurity, forgetfulness,
Unconsciousness, laziness, and bewilderment,
One wanders as an unprotected animal as a result.
Through the aspiration of myself, the buddha,
May the light of lucid mindfulness arise
In the obscurity of torpid bewilderment.
May nonconceptual wisdom be attained.

All beings of the three realms
Are equal to myself, the buddha, in the all-ground.
It became the ground of mindless confusion.
Now, they engage in pointless actions.
The six actions are like the bewilderment of dreams.
I am the first buddha.
I tame the six types of beings through emanations.
Through the aspiration of Samantabhadra,
May all beings without exception
Be awakened in the dharmadhātu.

❧ Attachment to Pleasure

THE PRAYER CONTINUES with verses that relate to the different poisons of the mind. These correlate with the psychological states of each of the six realms and with the different fundamental pain of each realm. The method to deal with the different poisons in each realm is discussed. The Prayer discusses the method to cut off the root cause of falling into that state of claustrophobia and then shows the wisdom nature of that klesha from the Dzogchen point of view.

Having previously discussed the subtle ignorances, which are the subtle level of causes, we come now to the coarse element of samsaric existence.

Dualism is doubt.

There is a basic sense of not clearly perceiving any reality. It is a basic sense of unclarity. That unclarity is in the nature of doubt. If you think clearly, unclarity is doubt. Doubt arises from ignorance and is the nature of duality here. From that point of view, dualism is doubt and doubt seems to be the subtle nature of duality. In that dualism is the basic cause of the coarse element of samsara.

From the emergence of subtle clinging
Coarse habit gradually develops.

These verses talk about the progression from the connate and labeling ignorances leading to the state of desire and attachment. The state of attachment develops from the repetitive action of the dualistic ignorance. It is not necessarily a conscious attachment, the mechanism just repeats again and again. This repeating of the same samsaric action of ignorance, again and again, is subtle craving. It is subtle attachment. From that subtle attachment develops the gross, intense, habitual clinging and habitual tendencies. Therefore, Samantabhadra begins by talking about the progression of this poison.

For example, you begin smoking by just doing it once. It's so innocent, it doesn't really matter. Out there with your friends there are no restrictions from rigpa, so you feel free. That one samsaric smoke leads to a second, which leads to a third. In the beginning, it's just the mechanism. We are just starting the movement, which itself has a subtle craving. A subtle attachment is developed in that subconscious move. That subconscious desire or craving grows into a very-difficult-to-give-up tendency. Passion, which is the difficult-to-give-up desire, is developed through that repetitive action.

> Food, wealth, clothing, places, companions,
> The five desirables, and beloved relatives—
> Beings are tormented by attachment to the pleasant.

Then we get tormented by lust. In the human realm, we crave food, wealth, clothing, home, and companions. These are just examples. It is important for us to be mindful of this passion and this attachment. We are talking about the craving for anything in the samsaric realm of desire.

Sometimes we feel that we don't have attachment to wealth, especially when we are poor. It's easy then. There is a saying, "The grapes that are very high on the vine are sour." We say that they are sour because they are very high up and we can't reach them. So it is very important for us to really look at our own minds to see what kind of attachments we have. We need to see the kinds of cravings with which we are weak in dealing.

Sometimes we have the misconception that we don't have such and such desire, such and such passion, or such and such craving. For example, a lot of people get shocked when you ask a monk or a nun whether he or she gets attracted to the opposite sex. People get really shocked if the answer is "Yes, I honestly do have this attraction." They say, "How can he or she have this?!" Actually, that's why he or she is a monastic. It is to try to overcome that desire. If any monastic says he or she doesn't have that desire or craving, it's a lie, unless he or she is a buddha or an arhat. We should not misjudge such things. It is very important to see that we all are going through these torments of lust, desire, and attachment, whether we are lay people or monastic, rich or poor. We all go through this, whatever level we are at and whatever state we are in.

Therefore, Samantabhadra says that we have attachment. We have attachment to food, wealth, clothing, home, companions, and loving friends. We have attachment to the five desirable sensory experiences, which are the objects of the five sensory perceptions. We are attached to beautiful forms, beautiful sounds, beautiful smells, beautiful tastes, and beautiful tactile sensations.

So the first thing that is dealt with here is attachment or desire. Attachment is actually the greatest suffering of all sentient beings. It is a little bit harder to recognize that because we always think suffering and pain come from hatred, anger, aggression, and so forth. But when you look at the suffering in the world, the suffering that arises from attachment is the worst. If you ask how many people have been hurt through aggression, through hatred, through some kind of fight or physical pain, there may be only a few. But if we ask how many of us have been hurt by passion, by attachment, or by desire, then all of us have been hurt—and not only once! We have all been hurt continuously by such desire and attachment.

Because beings are tormented by attachment to the pleasant, Shantideva said that samsaric pleasure is like honey on a razor blade. When we lick the honey, it's very sweet, very tasty, and very pleasant. But we forget that the sharp edge of the razor is just underneath the honey.

That is mundane confusion.
There is no end to the actions of dualism.

This means that our perceptions of the objects of the five sensory perceptions, as well as our conceptual experiences, are simply delusion. It's saying that they are all delusion, which is illusion. It's simply our mind. There is nothing called beautiful outside. Even in our mundane wisdom, we have the saying that beauty lies in the eye of the beholder. Usually, we've been very successful in ignoring that wisdom. That success leads to endless exhaustion, like being a successful lawyer.

❧ Fruit of Clinging

HAVING DISCUSSED how this basic ignorance develops into the poisonous mindstream that leads to different sufferings, Samantabhadra says,

> *When the fruit of clinging ripens,*
> *Born as pretas tormented by craving—*
> *How sad is their hunger and thirst.*

When the poison of mind called "attachment" or "desire" arises, the result is that we carry out many different actions. But it's not simply craving or desire, the main emotion here is passion, attachment. With that attachment, we commit actions of aggression, jealousy, pride, and so forth. Such actions bring the result of a lower birth.

One can cling to material objects as well as emotions. Clinging on to something, and not being able to let go, becomes a cause for taking birth in the state of a preta, a hungry ghost. In the hungry ghost realm, there is a continuous struggle. It is usually depicted with images of different tortured spirits.

The hungry ghost realm is a tremendously claustrophobic situation of psychological torture. It is filled with the pain of hunger and thirst, which refers to an extreme poverty mentality. No matter how much you have, no matter how much you possess, you still feel incomplete.

You still feel hunger, thirst, and desire. If we become too attached, if there is too much strong clinging to our objects of desire, the negative result of such clinging can become the experience of the hungry ghost realm.

You can see that in the stock market. One minute, a hundred thousand dollars is not enough. Then a million is not enough, then a billion, and it goes on and on. One day, the market crashes and you're left with nothing, not even enough to pay your rent and utility bills. It's like the experience of the hungry ghost realm. Too much desire, too much attachment and clinging, too much extreme poverty mentality or extreme dissatisfaction can lead us to the experience of this hungry ghost state.

This realm is an endless journey of desire. In this realm, you are unable to utilize whatever it may be that you possess. You are unable to use even one percent of it. In that very moment, you are still looking for something else, more and more and more and more.

In the hungry ghost realm, we build up a habitual tendency of clinging, of miserliness, of stinginess. Craving involves clinging on to something and not being able to let go. For example, we usually don't want to give happiness. We want to hold on to it. If you have some possession that you feel stingy about, you hold on to it, which builds up another habit.

The habit is a mechanical process. We develop that same tendency of holding on to something, whether it is to good things like happiness or to bad things such as anger and jealousy. At a certain point, we unknowingly develop this mechanistic sense of clinging. Desire goes to the root of our bad tendencies. We are not willing to let go of our bad tendencies because of this hunger, this desire. We are not willing to let go because of the clinging.

One aspect of the hungry ghost mentality is strongly present in human consciousness. Buddha said that one of the sufferings in the human realm is the poverty mentality, which is one of the biggest problems in the hungry ghost realm as well. This poverty mentality is very natural for human beings.

Because the poverty mentality is very dangerous, it is important for us to recognize and work with it. If we fail to work with it, we bring the same mundane hang-ups and neuroses on our spiritual journey. When we are on this spiritual journey, we must be aware of the poverty mentality and overcome it. As the saying goes, the grass is always greener on the other side of the fence. When we look out of our window, we see our neighbor's pasture as much greener than ours. So we buy that neighbor's backyard. Then we see the next neighbor's yard and now that one looks better.

We can do that same thing in our spiritual journey. When we are practicing according to one lineage, or when we are practicing one method of meditation, then another looks better. If we are doing shamatha meditation, then vipashyana always looks better. Ngöndro, the preliminary practices of Vajrayana, always looks like a much higher and nicer practice when we are doing shamatha. So we try to jump to vipashyana or to ngöndro, and then, again, it's the same. Those vipashyana people look much nicer. They look as if they are progressing much better. So we flip back to vipashyana. When we are practicing Mahamudra, then Dzogchen always looks much greener. So we jump to Dzogchen. And again, it's the same. Our neurosis is still there and so Mahamudra again looks much greener. It's a never-ending back and forth journey that leads to endless exhaustion. Therefore, working with this poverty mentality is very important in the spiritual journey.

When we have one good master, another one always looks kinder. The other one always looks much more skilled, much more intelligent, and so on. Then we flip back and forth with our teachers, the same as we do with everything else. That is the totally chaotic path called the hungry ghost realm.

Working with that poverty mentality is a way to transcend the tremendous psychological torture of a hungry ghost. It is a way to transcend the torture of endless desire, endless passion, and endless need. The suffering of a hungry ghost, that endless wanting, is no satisfaction.

In classical Buddhist paintings, the hungry ghosts are sitting right next to a beautiful lake while, at the same time, they are burning inside with thirst. Even while they burn inside with thirst, they have this stinginess. They think that the water will be completely consumed if they drink, so they never drink. It is said that even if the hungry ghosts drink, they burn inside even more because they worry about losing this wealth of water. If we are not mindful, this hungry ghost psychological state can happen to us at any time. Therefore Samantabhadra says,

> *Through the aspiration of myself, the buddha,*
> *May desirous beings*
> *Not reject the longing of desire*
> *Nor accept the clinging of attachment.*

Our prayer is that all sentient beings suffering through the causes of lust, passion, attachment, or desire neither suppress them nor go under their power. Whenever lust, passion, attachment, or desire arises, the method given here is not to reject these emotions. It is to let them come, let them arise.

There is no need to suppress this emotion. There is nothing wrong with its appearance. The raw energy of lust and passion is in the state of buddha wisdom. The Prayer says that whenever they arise, we should not go under the power of the labeling process, the power of conceptualizing the raw energy of lust and passion.

We go through this experience of tremendous energy called passion. What usually happens is that we conceptualize it later. That conceptualization leads us into an endless chain of thoughts and an endless chain of labeling. That endless chain of thoughts and labeling leads us to all sorts of different emotions, such as anger and jealousy, that become problematic.

The method is not to go into that chain of the repetitive actions of our emotions and conceptualizations. Just simply experience the emotion, neither reject it nor accept it. The raw energy is simply experienced without any thought, without any labeling process. Just simply be in that space. The Prayer says that this brings the wisdom of perfect discernment, discriminating wisdom, which corresponds to the wisdom of the western buddha field of Amitabha.

The great Indian yogi Saraha said that an agitated mind, if left alone, becomes peaceful. The problem here is not the passion. It is not the lust nor is it the desire. The problem is that we are not leaving them alone. We are not letting them be what they are. We are disturbing them with the labeling process, the thought process. We are not letting lust be lust, we are not letting desire be desire, we are not letting passion be passion. Therefore, the mind becomes agitated.

Not rejecting the longing of desire is very important. The point is that after seeing the faults of desire, after seeing the negative impact of clinging, attachment, and passion, we sometimes go to the other extreme of completely rejecting desire. Rejecting here refers to the path of Hinayana, where there is a sense of completely running away from the pleasures of samsaric passion, samsaric desire, and samsaric joy. When practitioners of the Hinayana see pleasures, they get the Hinayana monastic tremble. When they see beautiful fruit, they dare not pick it up.

Rejecting desire in a Hinayana way is running away from desire. It is practiced through reflecting on the faults and negative aspects of desire such as the meditation on ugliness, impermanence, and so forth. Rejecting desire in a Mahayana way is based on emptiness. It is practiced through transcending desire, transcending attachment, through the meditation of bodhicitta, and what we call *juma dapu ting nge dzin*, illusionlike samadhi.

Bodhisattvas see all relative experiences as illusion, as a dreamlike mirage. They sometimes accept desire, passion, and other emotions, but they do so by way of seeing it as illusion. It is acceptance in a transcendent way by seeing it as egoless passion or egoless attachment. There is a certain sense of rejecting its rawness, which is the ruggedness of emotions. Therefore, rejecting here has two aspects, the Hinayana element of complete rejection and the Mahayana element of rejection that involves the notion of transcendence.

In the Vajrayana path, we sometimes pursue an aspect of the path that accepts desire, accepts passion, and accepts attachment. There are practices of intentionally generating passion and purposely activating attachment. These practices give rise to desire and passion as part of the Vajrayana path. It is said that the more powerfully you give rise to passion, the more powerfully the experience of great bliss manifests from the Vajrayana point of view. The Vajrayana idea is that right when the forest begins to burn, the wind becomes an aid to the fire.

Samantabhadra's aspiration is that sentient beings neither reject desire in such an extreme way nor accept the clinging of attachment.

> *By relaxing cognition as it is*
> *May their awareness take its seat.*

The Dzogchen point of view says that intentionally generating passion, attachment, or desire is not necessary. The Dzogchen way of dealing with our desire is to relax cognition as it is. Relaxing our mind in that passion, just as it is, is like the Mahamudra approach. It is just resting in that fundamental experience of passion.

In Dzogchen, the notion of passion as being something either to be rejected or accepted does not exist. At this level, the basic state of passion itself, the basic state of the mind of attachment and desire itself, is in the complete state of enlightenment. The aspiration here is to just let it rest in its own state. Letting awareness take its seat in desire is good enough. Just face the raw energy of desire nakedly without the elaborations of the Hinayana, Mahayana, or Vajrayana. The simplicity of just simply resting, simply being in it completely and fully, is the key to liberation from the Dzogchen point of view. Therefore, we're making these aspirations, saying,

May they attain the wisdom of discrimination.

The wisdom of discrimination is the nature of passion here. It shows the nature of the emotion and the nature of Dzogchen practice. It also shows where emotion leads if we get caught up in it: it leads to the realm of pretas.

You can leave it in its own state, whatever it is, and simply experience that. Then, as it says, let awareness take its seat. This means it is just going back to its natural state. You are simply letting it be what it is, which is in the nature of rigpa.

If one knows how to rest in this state of passion, one can attain liberation. We are making aspiration prayers in order that all sentient beings, including ourselves, attain this state of rigpa and the wisdom of perfect discernment. That is our prayer here.

The teachings concerning the other poisons are given in the same pattern as this. They change the poison, the realm, and the wisdom. Other than that, they deal with each emotion in exactly the same way.

Fruit of Aversion

THE NEXT ASPIRATION concerns aggression:

Through the emergence of a subtle, fearful cognition
Of externally-apparent objects
The habit of aversion grows.
Coarse enmity, beating, and killing are born.
When the fruit of aversion ripens,
How much suffering there is in hell through boiling and burning.

Even better! We are not just talking about aggression alone. All of
the other emotions are included, such as passion, jealousy, and so
forth. But the mature poison of the mind discussed here is aggression.

The Prayer says that our basic fear is the fear of losing. In the beginning, we develop a subtle fear towards certain external appearances
that we experience in everyday life, such as our pride, our name, or our
position. It is a subtle fear of the apparent object outside gaining more
power, more wealth, a higher position or job. This fear is connected to
our basic pride and basic jealousy. Of course, pride and jealousy will
come later, but all emotions are connected through this fear. Passion
is connected to aversion, aversion is connected to passion, and so
forth. There's an interrelationship between them.

From that fear, the habit of aversion grows. Ego's fundamental fear,
which we all have in samsara, is the beginning of our aggression. That

basic fear leads us into the gross element of aggression. From there, some kind of friction takes place. From that, more and more hatred develops.

In order to achieve and defend the ego-centered view, aggression becomes very powerful. It is a great tool for ego to secure its fear. That is the primary use of aggression. This again leads us into habitual tendencies, just like passion. When aggression leads to the gross element of fear, it becomes very gross physical violence, verbal violence, and mental violence. Body, speech, and mind become very violent.

From that violent mind comes violent action. Violent action leads one to the resultant stage of hatred. In Buddhism, the resultant stage of hatred is called the hell realm. The emotion of aggression or aversion leads us to the state of the hell realm, or the hell-of-a-realm. This realm is depicted by the iconography of burning and boiling. The iconography should not be taken literally, it is just a symbol. Within that basic symbol, there are two elements of suffering, hot and cold. Among the two, the hot burning element is emphasized because it is more connected to aggression and hatred.

According to the Mahayana and Vajrayana views, all of these realms are very much psychological. In both the Mahayana sutras and the Vajrayana tantras, they are spoken about as being very much our minds, very much our mental states. We are the creator of these states as well as the experiencer of these states. They are all symbolic in Buddhism. There is no outside entity ruling over the hell realm. There is no Lord of Death giving commands and making you suffer. Such experiences arise from aggression, the emotion of anger.

Our great Indian master Shantideva said, "Who has created this hot and burning ground of a hell realm? Who is making this fire, this eternal fire of the hell realm?" He said that there is no outer creator of the hell realm. It has no outer existence. As the Buddha said, it is all a creation of your mind. The pain that we see in the hell realm is the creation of our mind. From these statements, we can clearly see that the hell realm is a psychological trauma. It's a state where we get completely claustrophobic. We get totally burned in this fire of aggression.

Shantideva said that when your mind is disturbed, agitated by this poison of aggression, it is eternally burning. You can't sleep, even at night, because your mind is disturbed by this anger, by this hatred. You can't concentrate during the day, on your work or on your meditation, because your mind is still burning. This eternal fire of aggression is going on. Shantideva said that you are in the psychological trauma of a hell realm when you give birth to this aggression.

The aggression causes us to burn and boil ourselves until we become completely exhausted. We do this until we literally fall apart. We don't need a literal fire to burn, we don't need literal water to boil. Psychologically, we are burned and boiled with anger, with hatred, with aggression. That state of psychological pain is caused by aggression. Therefore, the hell realm image in Buddhism is the image of the intense pain of aggression.

Anger has an object that is disturbing. If something is disturbing, we usually want to move it away. For example, if something is disturbing on the television, we want to flip to another channel. Shantideva says that it is impossible to destroy your object of anger outside. But if you conquer just one enemy, your aggression, it is like conquering all the objects of this anger. It is conquering the whole enemy group. It is like covering the soles of your feet with leather. You don't have to cover the whole world with leather so that you can walk barefoot on it, just wear shoes. If you cover your feet with leather, it is like covering the whole world. If you want to destroy an object, look inside and find the true enemy, which is aggression. Conquer that.

Shantideva said that anger is very destructive. He said that one moment of hatred or anger can destroy the virtue of many eons. Many millions of years of virtue can be destroyed by one moment of anger. So anger seems to be a pretty dangerous emotion. It is like a very destructive computer virus. It wipes out all the data that you have been working on for years. We may have done virtuous work on our computer for many days, months, and years. But if our computer is not properly backed up with bodhicitta, the heart of enlightenment, then the virtue gets destroyed by this moment of anger. Similarly, one moment of anger, aggression, or hatred can wipe out the data of all the virtuous actions.

If you look at a very tiny moment of hatred, it is very destructive. Destructive here does not really refer to others. Obviously, it would be harmful to have thoughts of hatred toward those surrounding you, but it is much more harmful to yourself than to any other person. Hatred, whether it is towards oneself or others, becomes very intense, very torturous, and very claustrophobic. This psychological state is called the hell realm. It is basically a hell of an experience.

For this reason, and from the earlier statements of Shantideva, we can clearly understand that the hell realm is nothing outside this very paranoid mind that we have. It is nothing outside our very violent and aggressive mind that is full of hatred. Therefore, when we become totally engaged in emotions such as hatred or anger, we experience a hell realm.

This is important for us to understand. The Mahayana and Vajrayana views say that whatever we experience, whatever we perceive, is basically our own creation. There is no outer creation and no outer creator. The creator is right here. If we are seeing nice beautiful scenery, it is our own creation. If we are seeing a horrible world outside or a horrible experience inside, it is also our creation. It is our mind's experience. This is a very important element in these teachings.

To look at an example of how it becomes our own creation, how it does not really reflect the true reality of the outside world, consider how things are when we fall in love. In the beginning, everything is wonderful when we look at that person. The way they appear is so beautiful. The clothes that they wear are so beautiful, so well-fitting.

Whatever perfume they may be wearing is such a refreshing scent. Even when we see that person crying, it is still a beautiful sound. In the beginning, it is all beautiful.

But somewhere along the way, things change a little bit here and there, even though we are looking at the same person doing the same things. He or she may be wearing the same clothes that they wore a few months ago, or ten years ago, but they don't look so good. They are putting on the same perfume, but we have developed an allergy. So we sneeze instead of feeling refreshed. At this point, when we hear them crying, the sound is so irritating. It's irritating even when the person says something beautiful. It's worse than crying was in the beginning. It may be the same hairstyle, the same clothing, the same perfume, and the same words, but it's perceived so differently.

This is called mind-only experience. In Buddhism, when we talk about mind-only, it doesn't mean that the other person doesn't exist. What we are saying is that the way we perceive, the way we relate, the way we see phenomena, is very much our mind only. It is our creation. We are projecting outside and we are perceiving that projection. It's very much our perception only. It is our conception only. In the same way, this hell realm is a creation of our mind. We are projecting all these weird things outside and going through tremendous unnecessary pain. At this point, we make a similar aspiration as before:

> *Through the aspiration of myself, the buddha,*
> *When strong aversion arises*
> *In all beings of the six states,*
> *May it be relaxed without rejection or acceptance.*
> *Awareness taking its seat,*
> *May beings attain the wisdom of clarity.*

By the power of this prayer of the Samantabhadra Buddha, the primordial buddha that is inseparable from ourselves, from our basic rigpa, we pray that all sentient beings of the six realms recognize rigpa. We pray that they recognize the wisdom element of rigpa within hatred, within anger, and within this violent attitude of aggression. As before, the method is to not suppress our violent hatred and anger.

At this point, we ease our consciousness into its own sphere. This means that we simply rest in the nature of the raw energy of hatred. Rest in the raw energy of anger, in the raw energy of aggression. That resting is very important here. By simply resting in that state, our mind slowly resumes its own basic state of rigpa. When you realize that basic state of naked awareness, the wisdom of buddha will appear naturally. The radiant clarity of the mirrorlike wisdom is attained.

◈ Inflated Mind

THE NEXT ASPIRATION we make relates to the emotion of pride and shows the connection of pride with the wisdom of equanimity. The basic pattern is the same as with passion and aggression.

One's mind becoming inflated,
An attitude of superiority to others,
Fierce pride, is born.
One experiences the suffering of disputation.
When the fruit of that action ripens,
One is born as a god and experiences death and downfall.

In this case, pride and arrogance are our problem. In Buddhism, pride and arrogance begin with the simple notion of ego-clinging. The notion of "I," that very basic clinging on to oneself as the self of person, is called pride.

We can see that from the basic fundamental ignorance we have already developed the seed of pride. No matter how much we are in control of our pride, we still have it. We cannot deny that we have pride. Even if we say, "I don't have pride. I am very low-key, and I'm very moderate, blah blah blah," there is still strong pride.

It is important to be aware of this emotion called pride. It is very dangerous and destructive because it causes us to refrain from learning. It blocks us from improving ourselves. Having pride means the end of our growing, the end of our development. Whenever we have pride in our practice or study of dharma, that's the end of any development in that particular practice, or that particular knowledge. We have a saying in Tibetan, "If the pot is upside down, no matter how much water you try to pour in, you can't fill it." The water touches the pot, but just rolls off by the nature of it being upside down. It will not even seep in. In this way, pride becomes quite destructive in our spiritual journey as well as in our mundane development of wisdom.

When one's mind becomes inflated with different relative qualities of pride, we develop an attitude problem. Because of this pride, this arrogance, we have an attitude of superiority to others. Therefore, there is nothing more to learn. That is the definition of pride; an attitude of superiority to others. We get into the suffering of disputation because we feel superior. For that reason, rivalry is created. Quarreling and fighting with others is created from pride.

We always have the sense of seeing others' faults. Actually, we think we see someone's faults. We think that we are doing better than someone else and that we see his or her problem. Then, naturally, we get into disputation. It is exactly the same for everyone. As much as I am thinking like that while looking at someone, the other person is doing the same thing while looking at me! So there is naturally a clash between two individual beings. There is no doubt about it. If it's only in one direction, then there is no problem. The other person will accept it and say, "Okay, I've been very wrong and bad." But that's not the case. We know that both people are looking at each other with the same kind of inflated mind. When the fruit of the action of pride ripens, we experience the realm of the gods.

In the gods' realm, we have so much happiness. We have the joy of material wealth as well as the joy of samadhi meditation, the mental wealth. At the level of the gods' realm, according to Buddhism, it is said that we have developed tremendous pride. We have the pride of thinking we have achieved the highest state of wealth, of joy, of happiness, and of samadhi.

But there is a great experience of suffering in the realm of the gods. In this realm, there still is the tremendous suffering of decay and eventual death. It is said that gods can predict their death a week before it happens. They can see it. Everyone in the realm sees it. One week before their death, no one will come near them. They become totally isolated from the rest of the realm. Actually, one week in the gods' realm is a long, long time for humans. According to *The Words of My Perfect Teacher*, by Patrul Rinpoche, one day in the gods' realm is one hundred human years. So, one week is seven hundred years. Therefore, at the time of death, when that karma is finished and it's time to depart from the realm of the gods to somewhere less favorable, there is the experience of tremendous suffering.

When we think about it, seven days is a long time, isn't it? If we are enjoying something, time feels so short. But if we are experiencing a hard time, one hour feels so long. We keep looking at the sun to see if something is wrong outside! We can see for ourselves how these can be very psychological as well as physical experiences.

In the gods' realm, there is no genuine path to liberation. No matter how much material wealth we enjoy at that point, we are still within the range of samsaric fear. It is pervaded by samsaric fear.

It is also said that beings in this realm develop a wrong view towards cause and effect, towards the law of karma. Until the time of death, these beings thought they had reached some sense of liberation. Then they realize that they have to go back. At that point, they lose faith in karma. They think, "Oh, what we have understood so far was not correct." So they develop wrong views toward cause and effect that result in more suffering, more negative actions in the future. Therefore, this is known as one of the six realms, which are realms of suffering.

We are making the aspiration to recognize the nature of pride as being in the nature of rigpa, in the nature of buddha wisdom. We are aspiring to release oneself and others from the same pride. So we say,

> *Through the aspiration of myself, the buddha,*
> *May beings with inflated minds*
> *Relax cognition as it is.*
> *Awareness taking its seat,*
> *May they realize equality.*

The method is the same as before. The main thing that we need to learn is how to be in whatever state we are in. We need to learn to be in that state completely, honestly, and without trying to pretend to be something better or something different. At the same time, we acknowledge our own pride, passion, aggression, and so on. We are aware of that emotion. We recognize it. We learn to be in the raw state of the emotion itself, without altering it, without trying to be something else.

For example, a rose is a rose and a sunflower is a sunflower. If we just appreciate the rose as being a rose, it is beautiful. It has lots of good qualities. It has a lot of beauty in its own state. But whenever we try to change that rose into something else, the problem starts. Whenever we try to change one thing into something else, the problem starts. In this prayer, Dzogchen teaches us to remain in the natural state of whatever emotion we have. It is to be totally awake and totally aware in that natural state. Being in that natural state will accomplish everything because that itself is in the nature of buddhahood. We don't need anything else. If the nature is not in rigpa or not in the state of buddha, then why bother? That is the logic. Even if we try to change, it's not going to work.

⊰⊱ Continuous Struggle

THE NEXT ASPIRATION is related to the emotion of jealousy:

Through the habit of developed dualism,
From the agony of praising oneself and denigrating others,
Quarrelsome competitiveness develops.
Born as an asura, killed and mutilated,
One falls to hell as a result.

Jealousy arises from envy, as well as from other emotions such as passion, and becomes very disturbing itself. It leads into the very speedy cycle of competitiveness, the very suffering of fighting and quarreling out of jealousy. The main problem of jealousy is lack of appreciation. It has the essence of a hungry ghost element, always wanting more. That's what we call competitiveness, always wanting more than what we have.

If we let these thoughts of jealousy and competitiveness go wild, we get a negative result. We are born into the realm that is the result of jealousy, called the asura realm, which is also known as the demigods' or jealous gods' realm. The classical Buddhist iconography of this realm has a very big wish-fulfilling fruit tree. The roots of the tree are in the demigods' realm while the fruit on top of the tree is in the gods' realm. The demigods water the tree and do all the work to make it grow, while the gods always get the fruit. Therefore, they are always jealous of the gods' realm and always fighting for the fruit. They're always competing with the realm of the gods and not quite winning the war. They enter this continuous struggle of being killed and mutilated.

The jealous gods' realm has this suffering of always envying someone else's wealth, happiness, or joy, and then fighting for it out of jealousy. If we fall into that category, through the actions of our body, speech, and mind, then we are in the jealous gods' realm. Because of jealousy, this sense of competitiveness, we engage in aggressive actions. The aggressive actions of anger, hatred, and aversion eventually lead us to the result of being born in a hell of a realm.

This is very important for dharma practitioners. Please listen carefully. "Through the habit of developed dualism" we go through this agony. We go through a painful experience of praising and denigrating. Praising oneself directly or indirectly, and denigrating others directly or indirectly, is the continual process of struggle. From such activities, we get caught up in the quarrelsome competitiveness that develops on the basis of such actions.

For that reason, the path of buddhadharma has the practice of rejoicing. There are also practices called bodhicitta, compassion, and love. Sometimes we act as if we have never heard of these before. If we see any of our dharma brothers and sisters doing better than us, in terms of the path quality of practicing, we should rejoice. If someone accomplishes more than us in terms of finishing their ngöndro or doing Mahamudra, Dzogchen, or deity yoga practices, we should rejoice. We should have the thought of rejoicing in their merit. Buddha said that if you rejoice in the merit arising from whatever positive actions others may be involved in, you get the same merit. Isn't that great? I don't know why people want to suffer and struggle in doing such things when you can accomplish the same merit without doing them. Therefore, there's great merit if we rejoice.

In some sense, rejoicing itself is a complete practice. If someone is doing a great job helping other sentient beings, and you rejoice in that person's actions, it's the same as if we are doing them. But if we get caught up in this quarrelsome competitiveness, then we lose everything. Even when we engage in activities with a positive intention, there's not much of a path quality in it if we're getting intensely caught up in quarrelsome competitiveness.

It may be very difficult for you because you have grown up in this culture of capitalism. It is a culture of competitiveness, so there's a sense of instinctive competitiveness coming up all the time. The path here is just to work with it. When it comes up, you have to work with it. That's the whole point.

Again, when we have this emotion of jealousy ripening in our mind-stream, we should just simply watch it. We should not suppress it nor let our mind become completely overwhelmed by the jealousy. We should maintain our balance and watch the nature of jealousy. Therefore, we make the aspiration that,

> *Through the aspiration of myself, the buddha,*
> *May those who quarrel through competitiveness*
> *Relax their enmity.*
> *Awareness taking its seat,*
> *May they attain the wisdom of unimpeded activity.*

This is a very nice prayer. When you do this prayer, think about your own klesha of jealousy, your own kleshas of competitiveness, aggressiveness, and so forth. Pray that oneself and other beings that are suffering from the same kleshas be free from such thought of enmity, that they relax their mind and that awareness takes its seat.

⟡ Mindless Apathy

THE NEXT ASPIRATION relates to the poison of delusion:

Through the distraction of mindless apathy,
Through torpor, obscurity, forgetfulness,
Unconsciousness, laziness, and bewilderment,
One wanders as an unprotected animal as a result.

It's very clear that ignorance becomes the root of all problems. Ignorance has the quality of not knowing what to adopt and what to relinquish. Ignorance is not just being unmindful, it doesn't have the sharpness to see the situation clearly.

Mindless apathy is the first aspect of delusion, so to speak. Torpor is that sense of being very heavy, very thick in terms of clarity. Obscurity is not seeing the nature directly. It is not seeing things directly or clearly. And forgetfulness, I don't remember. Here, "unconsciousness" refers to the literal meaning of unconsciousness, such as fainting and similar experiences.

Laziness is usually seen as the opposite of exertion or diligence. In Buddhism, exertion or diligence is taking delight in positive action, whether it's mental or physical. So the general sense of laziness is not taking delight in any positive or beneficial actions. In other words, the reason we are not taking delight in certain positive actions is that we're attached to some negative actions. For example, we're attached to sleep so we don't take delight in waking up, and so forth. In this way, some attachments to negative actions manifest as laziness. Bewilderment is like ignorance.

The negative result of these actions is that one wanders as an unprotected animal. In the animal realm, the poison of bewilderment leads us to the state of complete heaviness. In the animal realm, this kind of ignorance is very much present. The unprotected state of animal mind is, in some sense, completely dark and full of fear.

There's a lot more danger in the animal realm than the human realm. Just turn on the Discovery Channel. We can see right away that someone's eating someone else all the time, twenty-four hours a day. In the animal realm, we can see this more clearly than ever because of all the scientists doing research on different animal species. We can see the kind of situation they live in. There's a complete sense of danger and a lot of fear all the time.

On a certain level, animals don't see situations clearly. This doesn't mean that the animals don't perceive. It doesn't mean the animals don't know anything. It means that they don't know the crucial thing: they don't know what is to be adopted or what is to be relinquished.

Ignorance leads us to the result of taking birth in this psychological state in which there is the lack of sharpness. So, in a similar way, we apply the methods presented here. In the Dzogchen manner of practice, neither rejecting nor accepting, just simply rest in this poison. We make the aspiration to free ourselves and others from such ignorance that lacks the sharpness of discriminating wisdom:

> *Through the aspiration of myself, the buddha,*
> *May the light of lucid mindfulness arise*
> *In the obscurity of torpid bewilderment.*
> *May nonconceptual wisdom be attained.*

This is an important aspiration, because we all have this very strong animal quality of ignorance. It is important to aspire that our minds are not always spaced out. It is important to pray that our minds get more concentration, more sharpness, more on-the-point-of-dharma discernment. It is important to pray that our minds have the wisdom to realize the nature of rigpa within this ignorance.

According to the Vajrayana path of Dzogchen, even the nature of ignorance is in the nature of awareness. So, without altering the state of ignorance, without altering that state of unmindfulness, just simply look at the nature of this unmindfulness. Looking at the simple truth of basic ignorance, one will find the enlightened radiant clarity of mindfulness within the darkness of unmindfulness. In order to take this onto the path, we have many different practices such as the practice of luminosity, which uses the deep state of sleep as the path. This clearly shows that the nature of ignorance is in the nature of luminosity.

Question: You explained that in Tantra transcending disturbing emotions means not avoiding them. Can you explain how it is possible to stay, for example, in the emotion of hate with nothing less and nothing more?

Rinpoche: The true state of hatred, when you experience anger very strongly, is beyond concept. It's just an experience. It is like a vibration that you feel inside. When it is really strong, there is no concept at all. That's why no actions are very logical when they arise from anger. They are very stupid. If you look at them after a few hours, a few days, or a few weeks, you will see how stupid they were. That is because they were coming out of total nonsense.

What we are saying here is to just remain in that vibration of anger, which is almost like a complete shock. It is like any kind of shocking experience, like a roller coaster, or like Splash Mountain when you get totally soaked by the splashing water. Anger has the same kind of quality. It's very awakening in its nature but we usually paint it more than it requires or needs. We have to simply experience it.

When you experience it, just experience it. Just rest in it. Don't hate it and don't follow it with any more thoughts, any more paintings. Just be. Just sort of let it be. It comes close to the end of words at a certain point.

Buddha said that working with your emotions is like being a warrior on a battlefield. Emotions are like your enemy at this stage. You are the warrior. If you see that the enemy's troops are stronger, more skilled, and much bigger than yours, then the first method is to run. Run away rather than be stupid and get killed in the name of bravery. That's what the Vinaya path in the basic Hinayana journey is all about.

We do not run away completely: we run back to our training center. We get more training and build up our skills and power. We do this by our meditation. We retreat into monastic cells and meditate. We build up the power of our remedies and then come back to fight. When you are ready and know that you are going to conquer the enemy, then go ahead. In the basic Hinayana and Mahayana journey, it's like fighting on the battlefield. You are dealing with one individual soldier after another. There is a lot of detail work. A lot of conquering is required.

In Tantra, Buddha taught that the easiest way to win this war is to simply conquer the king. Once you do that, you don't have to go onto a battlefield and worry about individual details. When you conquer the king, you have conquered the whole army. So the Vajrayana method is slightly different.

Q: Every time I try to conquer the king, I get halfway there and then all the thousand soldiers come up within me. Do you think it is advisable to try to conquer the king, and then, if I see that I can't manage, to go back to counting breaths or some other method?

R: When you think about conquering the king, you can obviously see that there is a sophisticated protection barrier built up around him. It is like the Secret Service. Conquering the king requires a lot of skillful means and wisdom, prajna and upaya. That prajna and upaya are something that we learn in Vajrayana.

So, before you can conquer the king, you need to do a little research. You need to know how the guards are positioned and so forth. Then we can apply the method more effectively, and it will work. Therefore, going back to counting breaths sounds good. Then you can get additional methods to apply in a particular situation. It's very hard to generalize here. It is like trying to make a program that will work both on Mac and PC. It's quite challenging. There are different methods to apply to each of the different disturbances we have. When we apply the methods and work with the skillful means of the Vajrayana, then we can conquer the king. But it's a matter of your skillfulness, it's a matter of the sharpness of your prajna.

Q: Rinpoche, you said we should accept ignorance as it is, but we don't even recognize it because there is no discrimination. It's like being in a fog. Do you have any further suggestions?

R: On the one hand, ignorance is difficult to see. It is subtle, so it is hard to recognize. On the other hand, it's not that difficult, as we are often ignorant in handling situations. Because we are not skillful, when we fail to deal with an emotion and work with the disturbances, we can clearly see ignorance. We are ignorant in method, in wisdom, and in transcending this emotion or poison. Whenever you see strong ego-clinging, that is ignorance. It's very obvious.

As for the method, we have a tradition in Mahayana practice of reviewing the whole day. Every evening in our last session of meditation, we review the whole day. We try to think about the major emotional events that occurred during the day. We recollect whether we had a major anger, a major passion, or a major experience of hatred during that day. Then we really try to see it and we try to see how we handled it. Maybe we were somewhat successful, maybe we failed. We also try to see how many positive thoughts we had. See how many good thoughts that we had, such as thoughts of compassion. If we do that in our last meditation, we can see our ignorance pretty clearly. We can see our ignorance in these experiences of screwing up our opportunities to recognize rigpa. By reflecting, we can try to recognize ignorance.

Q: Dullness seems like the opposite of feeling naked, but I was wondering if dullness could be felt in a naked way.

R: Absolutely. That's why even the very extreme dullness of deep sleep is also taken onto the path in the Vajrayana. There's a way in which we try to realize luminosity in that very experience of dullness, in that very experience of complete ignorance, so to speak. All five poisons are actually taken onto the path as a completely enlightening experience, an awakening instruction or transmission. In some sense, these transmissions are received through our so-called neuroses, with some kind of basic enlightened twist.

PART SEVEN

Conclusion

All beings of the three realms
Are equal to myself, the buddha, in the all-ground.
It became the ground of mindless confusion.
Now, they engage in pointless actions.
The six actions are like the bewilderment of dreams.
I am the first buddha.
I tame the six types of beings through emanations.
Through the aspiration of Samantabhadra,
May all beings without exception
Be awakened in the dharmadhātu.

A HO
From now on whenever a powerful yogin
Within lucid awareness without bewilderment
Makes this powerful aspiration,
All beings who hear it
Will be fully awakened within three lives.

When the sun or moon is grasped by Rāhu,
When there is clamor or earthquakes,
At the solstices or at the year's change,
If he generates himself as Samantabhadra

And recites this in the hearing of all,
All beings of the three realms
Will be gradually freed from suffering
And will finally attain buddhahood
Through the aspiration of that yogin.

From the *Tantra of the Great Perfection Which Shows the Penetrating Wisdom of Samantabhadra,* this is the ninth chapter, which presents the powerful aspiration which makes it impossible for all beings not to attain buddhahood.

⤷⊀ Concluding Aspirations

All beings of the three realms
Are equal to myself, the buddha, in the all-ground.
It became the ground of mindless confusion.

THIS SUMMARIZES THE WHOLE PRAYER. In a way, Samantabhadra is saying that the true nature of the mind of all beings of the three worlds of samsara, including all six realms, is not different from him. The true nature of our mind is not separable from the heart of Samantabhadra. That is the nature. That is the ground of all.

As we discussed, the three realms are the realms of desire, form, and formlessness. Another way to look at it is to see the desire realm as the realm of apparent body, which is physical existence. It is the physical world that we experience in connection to our body. The realm of form is more like our speech, which is half physical and half nonsubstantial. The realm of formlessness is the realm of our mind. So, if you look at the three realms in connection to our own existence, they are body, speech, and mind from the Tantric point of view.

Whether we look at it from the Abhidharma or the Dzogchen point of view, all beings of the three realms are all equal to the Samantabhadra Buddha in the all-ground. "In the all-ground" refers to the ground of alaya, in which we're all equal. It is the same as buddha nature theory. The ground of alaya is in the state of alayajnana, which has the same nature as the wisdom of kadak. Therefore, Dzogchen says that samsara is in Samantabhadra nature and nirvana is in Samantabhadra nature. Samsara is alpha-pure and nirvana is alpha-pure. Samsara is all-good and primordially pure. Nirvana is all-good and primordially pure. There is no difference. They're all the same in the one ground. However, that one ground becomes the ground of mindless confusion for samsaric beings when they fail to recognize it.

> *Now, they engage in pointless actions.*
> *The six actions are like the bewilderment of dreams.*

As we discussed earlier, going from the unconscious state to that terrified blurry cognition, to the innate ignorance, to the labeling ignorance, and so forth, bewildered beings engage in many pointless actions as a result of such confusion. The six actions of the six kleshas lead to the six states of beings, and the six samsaric realms. All of these actions result from bewilderment, which is in the nature of a dream, illusory and nonsubstantial.

Because of ignorance, because of ego-clinging, we have the delusion of the six realms that is like a dream. Therefore, we make this aspiration that beings who are going through the dreamlike illusion of the six realms realize this manifestation of rigpa. We are making the aspiration that they come back to their original primordial state of Samantabhadra, the primordial state of rigpa, and so attain buddhahood. Attaining buddhahood is the attainment of rigpa, which is the attainment of the intrinsic nature of our mind.

> *I am the first buddha.*
> *I tame the six types of beings through emanations.*

When Samantabhadra says, "I am the first buddha," it means the primordial buddha. It also refers to our nature of mind. If you look at the nature of mind, it is primordially in the state of buddha, in the state of awakened heart.

When Samantabhadra says, "I tame the six types of beings through emanations," it refers to the forty-two peaceful and sixty wrathful emanations and, specifically, to taming beings in the six realms. According to Dzogchen, there is a different buddha that manifests in each realm. There is a buddha of the human realm, a buddha of the animal realm, and so on. There are different buddhas to tame beings of the different realms. Therefore, once again,

> *Through the aspiration of Samantabhadra,*
> *May all beings without exception*
> *Be awakened in the dharmadhātu.*

Our whole aspiration is that all sentient beings come back to their original state of buddhahood. We begin our journey from there and we come back to square one, which is rigpa.

⫷ The Benefit

A HO
From now on, whenever a powerful yogin
Within lucid awareness without bewilderment
Makes this powerful aspiration,

I N THE BEGINNING, we said "HO." This is "A HO," which has the same quality of expressing the joy, appreciation, satisfaction, wondrous activities of Samantabhadra, and so forth. That's the benefit of this aspiration. Isn't that great? It's a jolly good prayer here, a marvelous prayer.

If you're a completely dedicated practitioner, it is bound to bring some realization. When one has realization, one is a powerful yogin. So, when you do this prayer, the instruction is to rest your mind in this lucid, vivid, and vibrating awareness. Rest in the basic clarity without bewilderment. Rest within that mindfulness and make this powerful aspiration. It is the aspiration of Samantabhadra that when this prayer is made by a powerful yogin,

All beings who hear it
Will be fully awakened within three lives.

If someone is liberated within three lifetimes just from hearing this aspiration, if we study it, clearly contemplate it, and do it with full mindfulness and awareness, then the benefit is immeasurable. It is beyond any limit.

When it says liberation will occur within three lifetimes, that's a very Tantric expression. From the Vajrayana point of view, if we connect to this path of Vajrayana, we have a great chance of attaining the fully awakened state of buddhahood in this lifetime. If we screw up our Vajrayana path a little bit, then maybe it will take three lifetimes. If we screw up even more on this Vajrayana path, then it will take seven lifetimes. In a way, this means that if we practice, we are guaranteed to achieve enlightenment within, at most, seven lifetimes. Of course, the key is practicing according to the instruction of the guru. If we don't attain enlightenment in seven lifetimes, it means there is serious damage to our samaya.

This prayer says "within three lives" because once someone hears such a Tantric aspiration, that person makes a karmic connection to the Vajrayana path. When one makes the connection to the Vajrayana path, that person might get connected in this lifetime. In this lifetime, that person might practice the Vajrayana path and attain some kind of awakening realization. But if not in this lifetime, then the Prayer says that it will occur within three lifetimes. This part shows a path for those who are not interested in an elaborate idea of practice. Just practice this aspiration in everyday life, maintain such awareness in everyday life.

The final section of the Prayer shows exactly when to do this prayer. For those who are elaborate practitioners in the relative sense,

> *When the sun or moon is grasped by Rāhu,*
> *When there is clamor or earthquakes,*
> *At the solstices or at the year's change,*
> *If he generates himself as Samantabhadra*
> *And recites this in the hearing of all,*
> *All beings of the three realms*

Will be gradually freed from suffering
And will finally attain buddhahood
Through the aspiration of that yogin.

If you don't do this prayer every day, or if you don't practice it frequently, then you can do it at the time of the solar eclipses, or any special day, like a birthday, death day, or whatever. I think it is good to do on eclipses, the full moon, or the new moon. If you have the time, then do it as often as you can.

The colophon explains the source of this Aspiration Prayer:

> From the *Tantra of the Great Perfection Which Shows the Penetrating Wisdom of Samantabhadra*, this is the ninth chapter, which presents the powerful aspiration which makes it impossible for all beings not to attain buddhahood.

Isn't that nice?

This aspiration has been taught for several reasons. First, I would like the sangha to make a deeper connection to the Dzogchen lineage. Therefore, instead of just presenting a general talk of my own creation, I thought it would be auspicious to discuss an authentic teaching of the Dzogchen tantras. Second, many students are already engaged in ngöndro practices, or are interested in engaging in ngöndro practices, so it's good to have some kind of direct teaching relating to rigpa, naked awareness, or ordinary mind. Third, for Vajrayana practitioners who have completed ngöndro, and are doing yidam, Mahamudra, or Dzogchen practices, this aspiration will be very nice to do.

If you are a Tantric practitioner, visualize yourself as Samantabhadra Buddha and recite this prayer with reflection on each point. Briefly speaking, that is how we can practice this prayer.

ཀུན་བཟང་སྨོན་ལམ།

༄ Kunzang Mönlam

ཀུན་བཟང་སྨོན་ལམ།

༄། །ཧོཿ

སྣང་སྲིད་འཁོར་འདས་ཐམས་ཅད་ཀུནཿ

གཞི་གཅིག་ལམ་གཉིས་འབྲས་བུ་གཉིསཿ

རིག་དང་མ་རིག་ཆོ་འཕྲུལ་ཏེཿ

ཀུན་ཏུ་བཟང་པོའི་སྨོན་ལམ་གྱིསཿ

ཐམས་ཅད་ཆོས་དབྱིངས་ཕོ་བྲང་དུཿ

མངོན་པར་རྫོགས་ཏེ་འཚང་རྒྱ་ཤོགཿ

ཀུན་གྱི་གཞི་ནི་འདུས་མ་བྱསཿ

རང་བྱུང་ཀློང་ཡངས་བརྗོད་དུ་མེདཿ

འཁོར་འདས་གཉིས་ཀའི་མིང་མེད་དོཿ

དེ་ཉིད་རིག་ན་སངས་རྒྱས་ཏེཿ

མ་རིག་སེམས་ཅན་འཁོར་བར་འཁྱམསཿ

ཁམས་གསུམ་སེམས་ཅན་ཐམས་ཅད་ཀྱིསཿ

བརྟེན་མེད་གཞི་དོན་རིག་པར་ཤོག༔

ཀུན་ཏུ་བཟང་པོ་ང་ཡིས་ཀྱང་༔

རྒྱུ་རྐྱེན་མེད་པ་གཞི་ཡི་དོན༔

དེ་ཉིད་གཞི་ལ་རང་བྱུང་རིག༔

ཕྱི་ནང་སྒྲོ་སྐུར་སྐྱོན་མ་བཏགས༔

དྲན་མེད་མུན་པའི་སྒྲིབ་མ་གོས༔

དེ་ཕྱིར་རང་སྣང་སྐྱོན་མ་གོས༔

རང་རིག་སོ་ལ་གནས་པ་ལ༔

སྲིད་གསུམ་འཇིགས་ཀྱང་དངངས་སྐྲག་མེད༔

འདོད་ཡོན་ལྔ་ལ་ཆགས་པ་མེད༔

རྟོག་མེད་ཤེས་པ་རང་བྱུང་ལ༔

རྡོས་པའི་གཟུགས་དང་དུག་ལྔ་མེད༔

རིག་པའི་གསལ་ཆ་མ་འགགས་པ༔

ངོ་བོ་གཅིག་ལ་ཡེ་ཤེས་ལྔ༔

ཡེ་ཤེས་ལྔ་པོ་སྨིན་པ་ལས༔

ཕྱོག་མའི་སངས་རྒྱས་རིགས་ལྔ་བྱུང་༔

དེ་ལས་ཡེ་ཤེས་མཐའ་རྒྱས་པས༔

སངས་རྒྱས་བཞི་བཅུ་རྩ་གཉིས་བྱུང་༔

ཡེ་ཤེས་ལྔ་ཡི་རྩལ་ཤར་བས༔

ཁྲག་འཐུང་དྲུག་ཅུ་ཐམ་པ་བྱུང་༔

དེ་ཕྱིར་གཞི་རིག་འཁྲུལ་མ་མྱོང་༔

ཕྱོག་མའི་སངས་རྒྱས་ང་ཡིན་པས༔

ང་ཡི་སྐྱོན་ལས་བཏབ་པ་ཡིས༔

ཁམས་གསུམ་འཁོར་བའི་སེམས་ཅན་ཀུན༔

རང་བྱུང་རིག་པ་རྡོ་ཤེས་ནས༔

ཨེ་ཤེས་ཆེན་པོ་མཐའ་རྒྱས་ཤོག༔

ང་ཡི་སྤྲུལ་པ་རྒྱུན་མི་ཆད༔

བྱེ་བ་ཕྲག་བརྒྱ་བསམ་ཡས་འགྱེད༔

གང་ལ་གང་འདུལ་སྐུ་ཙྩགས་སྟོན༔

ང་ཡི་ཐུགས་རྗེའི་སྨོན་ལམ་གྱིས༔

ཁམས་གསུམ་འཁོར་བའི་སེམས་ཅན་ཀུན༔

རིགས་དྲུག་གནས་ནས་འཐོན་པར་ཤོག༔

དང་པོ་སེམས་ཅན་འཁྲུལ་པ་རྣམས༔

གཞི་ལ་རིག་པ་མ་ཤར་བས༔

ཅི་ཡང་དྲན་མེད་ཐོམ་མེ་བ༔

དེ་ཀ་མ་རིག་འཁྲུལ་པའི་རྒྱུ༔

དེ་ལ་ཧད་ཀྱིས་བརྒྱལ་བ་ལས༔

དངངས་སྐྲག་ཤེས་པ་ཟ་ཟི་འགྱུས༔

དེ་ལས་བདག་གཞན་དགྲར་འཛིན་སྐྱེས༔

བག་ཆགས་རིམ་བཞིན་བརྟས་པ་ལས༔

འཁོར་བ་ལུགས་སུ་འཇུག་པ་བྱུང་༔

དེ་ལས་ཉོན་མོངས་དུག་ལྔ་རྒྱས༔

དུག་ལྔའི་ལས་ལ་རྒྱུན་ཆད་མེད༔

དེ་ཕྱིར་སེམས་ཅན་འཁྲུལ་པའི་གཞི༔

དྲན་མེད་མ་རིག་ཡིན་པའི་ཕྱིར༔

སངས་རྒྱས་ང་ཡི་སྨོན་ལམ་གྱིས༔

ཀུན་གྱི་རིག་པ་རང་ཤེས་གྲོག །

ལྷུན་ཅིག་སྐྱེས་པའི་མ་རིག་པ། །

ཤེས་པ་དྲན་མེད་ཡེངས་པ་ཡིན། །

ཀུན་ཏུ་བཏགས་པའི་མ་རིག་པ། །

བདག་གཞན་གཉིས་སུ་འཛིན་པ་ཡིན། །

ལྷུན་ཅིག་ཀུན་བཏགས་མ་རིག་གཉིས། །

སེམས་ཅན་ཀུན་གྱི་འཁྲུལ་གཞི་ཡིན། །

རང་རྒྱས་ང་ཡིས་སྨྲོན་ལམ་གྱིས། །

འཁོར་བའི་སེམས་ཅན་ཐམས་ཅད་ཀྱི། །

དུན་མེད་འཁྲིབ་པའི་མུན་པ་སངས། །

གཉིས་སུ་འཛིན་པའི་ཤེས་པ་དངས། །

རིག་པའི་རང་ངོ་ཤེས་པར་གྲོག །

གཉིས་འཛིན་བློ་ནི་ཞི་ཚོམ་སྟེ། །

ཞེན་པ་ཕྲ་མོ་སྐྱེས་པ་ལས། །

བག་ཆགས་འཕྲུག་པོ་རིམ་གྱིས་བརྟས། །

ཟས་ནོར་གོས་དང་གནས་དང་གྲོགས། །

འདོད་ཡོན་ལྔ་དང་བྱམས་པའི་གཉེན། །

ཡིད་འོང་ཆགས་པའི་འདོད་པས་གདུངས། །

དེ་དག་འཛིག་སྟེན་འཁྲུལ་པ་སྟེ། །

གཟུང་འཛིན་ལས་ལ་ཟད་མཐའ་མེད། །

ཞེན་པའི་འབྲས་བུ་སྐྱིན་པའི་ཚེ། །

ཀྲམ་ཆགས་གདུང་བའི་ཡི་དགས་སུ། །

སྐྱེས་ནས་བཀྲེས་སྐོམ་ཡ་རེ་ང༌། །

སངས་རྒྱས་ང་ཡི་སྨོན་ལམ་གྱིས༔

འདོད་ཆགས་ཞེན་པའི་སེམས་ཅན་རྣམས༔

འདོད་པའི་གདུང་བ་ཕྱིར་མ་སྤངས༔

འདོད་ཆགས་ཞེན་པ་ཆུར་མ་བླུང༔

ཤེས་པ་རང་སོར་གྱོད་པ་ཡིས༔

རིག་པ་རང་སོ་ཟིན་གྱུར་ནས༔

ཀུན་རྟོག་ཡེ་ཤེས་ཐོབ་པར་ཤོག༔

ཕྱི་རོལ་ཡུལ་གྱི་སྣང་བ་ལ༔

འཇིགས་སྐྲག་ཤེས་པ་ཕྲ་མོ་འགྱུས༔

སྡང་བའི་བག་ཆགས་བརྟས་པ་ལས༔

དགྲར་འཛིན་བརྡེག་གསོད་དྲག་པ་སྐྱེས༔

ཞེ་སྡང་འབྲས་བུ་སྨིན་པའི་ཚེ༔

དམྱལ་བའི་བཙོ་བསྲེག་སྡུག་རེ་བསྔལ༔

སངས་རྒྱས་ཡེ་ས་སྨོན་ལམ་གྱིས༔

འགྲོ་དྲུག་སེམས་ཅན་ཐམས་ཅད་ཀྱི༔

ཞེ་སྡང་དྲག་པོ་སྐྱེས་པའི་ཚེ༔

སྐྱང་བྲང་མི་བྱ་རང་སོར་ཀློད༔

རིག་པ་རང་སོ་ཟིན་གྱུར་ནས༔

གསལ་བའི་ཡེ་ཤེས་ཐོབ་པར་ཤོག༔

རང་སེམས་ཁེངས་པར་གྱུར་པ་ལ༔

གཞན་ལ་འགྲན་སེམས་སྐྱེད་པའི་བློ༔

ང་རྒྱལ་དྲག་པོའི་སེམས་སྐྱེས་པས༔

བདག་གཞན་འཐབ་རྩོད་སྡུག་བསྔལ་སྐྱོང་༔

ལས་ངེའི་འབྲས་བུ་སྨིན་པའི་ཚེ༔

འཕོ་ལྡང་སྐྱོང་བའི་ལྷ་རུ་སྐྱེ༔

སངས་རྒྱས་ང་ཡི་སྨོན་ལམ་གྱིས༔

ཁྱེད་སེམས་སྐྱེས་པའི་སེམས་ཅན་རྣམས༔

དེ་ཚེ་ཤེས་པ་རང་སོར་ཀློད༔

རིག་པ་རང་སོ་ཟིན་གྱུར་ན༔

མཉམ་པ་ཉིད་ཀྱི་དོན་རྟོགས་ཤོག༔

གཉིས་འཛིན་བཏུས་པའི་བག་ཆགས་ཀྱིས༔

བདག་བསྐྱེད་གཞན་སྐྱེད་རྒྱག་ཏུ་ལས༔

འཐབ་རྩོད་འགྲན་སེམས་བཏུས་པ་ལས༔

གསོད་གཅོད་ལྷ་མིན་གནས་སུ་སྐྱེ༔

འབྲས་བུ་དམྱལ་བའི་གནས་སུ་ལྷུང་༔

སངས་རྒྱས་ང་ཡི་སྨོན་ལམ་གྱིས༔

འགྲན་སེམས་འཐབ་རྩོད་སྐྱེས་པ་རྣམས༔

དགྲ་འཛིན་མི་བྱ་རང་སོར་ཀློད༔

ཤེས་པ་རང་སོ་ཟིན་གྱུར་ནས༔

ཕྲིན་ལས་ཐོགས་མེད་ཡེ་ཤེས་ཤོག༔

དྲན་མེད་གཏི་མུག་སྦོམས་ཡེངས་པ་ཡིས༔

འཐིབས་དང་རྨུགས་དང་བརྗེད་པ་དང་༔

བརྒྱལ་དང་ལེ་ལོ་གཏི་མུག་ལས༔

འབྲས་བུ་སྐྱབས་མེད་བྱོལ་སོང་འཁྱམས༔

སངས་རྒྱས་ང་ཡི་སྨོན་ལམ་གྱིས༔

གཏི་མུག་བྱིངས་པའི་མུན་པ་ལ༔

དྲན་པ་གསལ་བའི་མདངས་ཤར་བས༔

རྟོག་མེད་ཡེ་ཤེས་ཐོབ་པར་ཤོག༔

ཁམས་གསུམ་སེམས་ཅན་ཐམས་ཅད་ཀུན༔

ཀུན་གཞི་རང་རྒྱས་ང་དང་མཉམ༔

དྲན་མེད་འཁྲུལ་པའི་གཞི་རུ་སོང་༔

ད་ལྟ་དོན་མེད་ལས་ལ་སྤྱོད༔

ལས་དྲུག་རྨི་ལམ་འཁྲུལ་ལ་འདྲ༔

ང་ནི་སངས་རྒྱས་ཐོག་མ་ཡིན༔

འགྲོ་དྲུག་སྤྲུལ་པས་འདུལ་བའི་ཕྱིར༔

ཀུན་ཏུ་བཟང་པོའི་སྨོན་ལམ་གྱིས༔

སེམས་ཅན་ཐམས་ཅད་མ་ལུས་པ༔

ཆོས་ཀྱི་དབྱིངས་སུ་འཚང་རྒྱ་ཤོག༔

ཨ་ཧོ༔

ཕྱིན་ཆད་རྣལ་འབྱོར་སྟོབས་ཅན་གྱིས༔

འཁྲུལ་མེད་རིག་པ་རང་གསལ་ནས༔

སྨོན་ལམ་སྟོབས་ཅན་འདི་བཏབ་ལས༔

འདི་ཐོས་སེམས་ཅན་ཐམས་ཅད་ཀུན༔

སྐྱེ་བ་གསུམ་ནས་མངོན་འཚང་རྒྱ༔

ཉི་ཟླ་གཟའ་ཡིས་ཟིན་པའམ༔

སྒྲ་དང་ས་གཡོས་བྱུང་བའམ༔

ཉི་མ་ལྡོག་འགྱུར་ལོ་འཕོ་དུས༔

རང་ཉིད་ཀུན་ཏུ་བཟང་པོར་བསྐྱེད༔

ཀུན་གྱིས་ཐོས་པར་འདི་བརྗོད་ནཿ

ཁམས་གསུམ་སེམས་ཅན་ཐམས་ཅད་ལཿ

རྣལ་འབྱོར་དེ་ཡི་སྨོན་ལམ་གྱིསཿ

སྲུག་བསྲལ་རིམ་བཞིན་གྲོལ་ནས་ཀྱངཿ

མཐའ་རུ་སངས་རྒྱས་ཐོབ་པར་འགྱུརཿ

ཞེས་གསུངས་སོ། །རྟོགས་པ་ཆེན་པོ་ཀུན་ཏུ་བཟང་པོའི་དགོངས་པ་ཟང་ཐལ་དུ་བསྟན་པའི་རྒྱུད་ལས། སྨོན་ལམ་སྟོབས་པོ་ཆེ་བཏབ་པས་སེམས་ཅན་ཐམས་ཅད་སངས་མི་རྒྱ་བའི་དབང་མེད་པར་བསྟན་པའི་ལེའུ་དགུ་པ་ཁོལ་དུ་ཕྱུངས་པའོ།། །།

Glossary

Abhisheka (Skt) — དབང་ [T: dbang] *(wang)*; empowerment.

Absolute truth — དོན་དམ་བདེན་པ་ [T: don dam bden pa] *(döndam denpa)*; the nature of all things, beyond any and all elaborations, unfabricated by confused, conflicted, or ignorant cognition.

Alaya (Skt) — ཀུན་གཞི་[T: kun gzhi] *(kun-shi)*; all-basis, the mind stream. When this is not recognized, it is called all-basis consciousness, alayavijnana (Skt), ཀུན་གཞི་རྣམ་པར་ཤེས་པ་ [T: kun gzhi rnam par shes pa] *(kun-shi nampar shepa)*. When it is recognized, it is called all-basis wisdom or connate wisdom, alayajnana (Skt), ཀུན་གཞིའི་ཡེ་ཤེས་ [T: kun gzhi'i ye shes] *(kun-shi yeshe)*. NG

Amitabha (Skt) — འོད་དཔག་མེད་ [T: 'od dpag med] *(ö-pak me)*; the buddha of the western direction.

Amoghasiddhi (Skt) — དོན་ཡོད་གྲུབ་པ་ [T: don yod grub pa] *(dönyö druppa)*; the buddha of the northern direction.

Anuyoga (Skt) — The eighth yana in the nine-yana journey.

Asanga — ཐོགས་མེད་ [T: thogs me] *(thogme)*; he received the Uttaratantra teachings on buddha nature from Maitreya Buddha.

Ashoka (Skt) — A great dharma king in Uddiyana, grandfather of Garab Dorje. The name Ashoka often refers to the dharma king in India that built the stupa in Sarnath, India, at the site of Shakyamuni Buddha's first turning of the wheel of dharma.

Ati or Atiyana (Skt) — Ninth yana in the Dzogchen tradition, full realization in the Dzogchen tradition. The ninth yana in the nine-yana journey. *See also* Dzogchen.

Bardo — བར་དོ་[T: bar do]; the intermediate state. Bardo generally refers to the state following death and before the next birth. NG

Bodhisattvayana (Skt) — བྱང་ཆུབ་སེམས་དཔའི་ཐེག་པ་[T: byang chub sems dpa'i theg pa] (changchub sempe thekpa); see Mahayana.

Buddha — སངས་རྒྱས་[T: sangs rgyas] (sangye); awakened, fully enlightened. See Shakyamuni.

Chandragomin — Indian master, disciple of Sthiramati (seventh century). NG

Chandrakirti — ཟླ་བ་གྲགས་པ་ [T: zla ba grags pa] (dawa drakpa); Indian master, one of the main disciples of Nagarjuna. NG

Chemchok — ཆེ་མཆོག [T: che mchog]; Mahottara Heruka, wrathful manifestation of Samantabhadra.

Chotrül — ཆོ་འཕྲུལ། [T: cho 'phrul]; magical display.

Connate wisdom — ལྷན་ཅིག་སྐྱེས་པའི་ཡེ་ཤེས། [T: lhan cig skyes pa'i ye shes] (lhenchig kye-pai yeshe); also translated as co-emergent or innate wisdom.

Connate ignorance — ལྷན་ཅིག་སྐྱེས་པའི་མ་རིག་པ། [T: lhan cig skyes pa'i ma rig pa] (lhenchig kye-pai ma rigpa); the innate ignorance or conception of a truly existing self that is common naturally to all beings. NG

Dakinis (Skt) — མཁའ་འགྲོ་མ། [T: mkha' 'gro ma] (khandroma); female Tantric deities who protect and serve the Buddhist doctrine and practitioners.

Dampa rik gya — དམ་པ་རིགས་བརྒྱ། [T: dam pa rigs brgya]; one hundred manifestations of deities connected with the bardo.

Denigration — སྐུར་འདེབས། [T: skur 'debs] (kur-deb); to deny the existence of something that does exist conventionally. See also Superimposition. NG

Dharma (Skt) — ཆོས། [T: chos] (chö); the teachings of the Buddha.

Dharmadhatu (Skt) — ཆོས་དབྱིངས། [T: chos dbyings] (chöying); the ultimate, primordial expanse of the phenomena of samsara and nirvana, which is nonarising and unceasing, unconditioned and unchanging. NG

Dharmakaya (Skt) — ཆོས་སྐུ། [T: chos sku] (chöku); the dharmakaya is the realization of the essence of vipashyana or the result of perfecting the nature of nonconceptuality. It is the fruition achieved for one's own benefit. It is also said that it is the nonarising of the mind itself and is free from all conceptual elaborations. NG. Dharmakaya is the state of the inseparability of wisdom and space, wisdom and expanse.

Dharmata — ཆོས་ཉིད། [T: chos nyid] *(chönyi)*; reality. The ultimate nature or reality of mind and phenomena. Synonymous with emptiness. NG

Dominating ignorance — The basic ignorance from which dualistic mind develops.

Dorje Sempa — རྡོ་རྗེ་སེམས་དཔའ། [T: rdo rje sems dpa']; *see* Vajrasattva.

Dzogchen — རྫོགས་ཆེན། [T: rdzogs chen]; great perfection, great completion, or great exhaustion. *See* Ati.

Eight tramen — ཕྲ་མེན། [T: phra men]; goddesses. The tramen goddesses are wrathful with human bodies and animal heads.

Emptiness — Shunyata (Skt), སྟོང་པ་ཉིད།[T: stong pa nyid] *(tongpa nyi)*; the ultimate nature of all things. The recognition that all composite things are without inherent existence.

Five desirables — འདོད་ཡོན་ལྔ། [T: 'dod yon lnga] *(dö yön nga)*; beautiful forms, pleasant sounds, fragrant scents, delicious tastes, and soft tangible objects. NG

Five kayas — སྐུ་ལྔ། [T: sku lnga] *(ku nga)*; dharmakaya, ཆོས་སྐུ། [T: chos sku] *(chöku)*; sambhogakaya, ལོངས་སྤྱོད་རྫོགས་པའི་སྐུ། [T: longs spyod rdzogs pa'i sku] *(longchö dzogpay ku)*; nirmanakaya, སྤྲུལ་སྐུ། [T: sprul sku] *(trulku)*; svabhavakaya, ངོ་བོ་ཉིད་ཀྱི་སྐུ། [T: ngo bo nyid kyi sku] *(ngo wo nyi kyi ku)*; and abhisambodhikaya, མངོན་པར་བྱང་ཆུབ་པའི་སྐུ། [T: mngon par byang chub pa'i sku] *(ngönpar jangchup payku)*.

Five luminous lights — འོད་ལྔ། [T: 'od lnga] *(ö nga)*; the luminous lights of rigpa are white, yellow, red, green, and deep blue.

Five poisons — དུག་ལྔ། [T: dug lnga] *(dug nga)*; the five poisonous mental afflictions are desire, aggression, ignorance, pride, and jealousy. NG

Five types of Kuntuzangpo — Completely pure teacher, སྟོན་པ་ཀུན་ཏུ་བཟང་པོ། [T: ston pa kun tu bzang po] *(tönpa kuntuzangpo)*; completely pure ornament, referring to the ornament of the teacher, which is his teachings, རྒྱན་ཀུན་ཏུ

བཟང་པོ། [T: rgyan kun tu bzang po] *(gyen kuntuzangpo)*; completely pure path, ལམ་ཀུན་ཏུ་བཟང་པོ། [T: lam kun tu bzang po] *(lam kuntuzangpo)*; completely pure awareness or bare naked awareness, རིག་པ་ཀུན་ཏུ་བཟང་པོ། [T: rig pa kun tu bzang po] *(rigpa kuntuzangpo)*; completely pure realization, རྟོགས་ པ་ཀུན་ཏུ་བཟང་པོ། [T: rtogs pa kun tu bzang po] *(togpa kuntuzangpo)*.

Five wisdoms — Dharmadhatu wisdom, the wisdom of seeing the true nature of phenomena, ཆོས་ཀྱི་དབྱིངས། [T: chos kyi dbyings] *(chökyi ying)*; mirrorlike wisdom, མེ་ལོང་ལྟ་བུའི་ཡེ་ཤེས། [T: me long lta bu'i ye shes] *(melong ta-bü yeshe)*; wisdom of equality, མཉམ་ཉིད་ཡེ་ཤེས། [T: mnyam nyid ye shes] *(nyam-nyi yeshe)*; discriminating awareness wisdom, སོ་སོར་རྟོག་པའི་ཡེ་ཤེས། [T: so sor rtog pa'i ye shes] *(so-sor tokpe yeshe)*; all-accomplishing wisdom, བྱ་བ་གྲུབ་ པའི་ཡེ་ཤེས། [T: bya ba grub pa'i ye shes] *(jawa drup-pe yeshe)*.

Four conditions — The causal condition is not recognizing the manifestation of ground as the luminosity aspect of the naked nature of our mind. The objective condition is the condition through which these delusions arise, i.e., mistaking luminosity for objects of samsaric perception. The dominating condition is ego-clinging. The instantaneous or immediate condition refers to the co-emergent nature of these previous three conditions together.

Gampopa — སྒམ་པོ་པ། [T: sgam po pa]; also known as Dakpo Rinpoche. Foremost disciple of Milarepa, he also studied with Kadampa teachers. His main disciples include Dusum Khyenpa (the first Gyalwang Karmapa) and Pakmo Drupa. (1079-1153). NG

Garab Dorje — The first human holder of the Dzogchen lineage.

Gaurima gye — གོ་རའི་མ་བརྒྱད། [T: goo ra'i ma brgyad] *(gaurima gye)*; eight yoginis.

Guru Rinpoche — *See* Padmasambhava.

Guru yoga — The practice of unifying one's mind with the mind of the guru.

Heruka — ཁྲག་འཐུང་། [T: khrag 'thung] *(thrag thung)*; literally translated as "blood drinker." Heruka is a more wrathful, more yogic style of a buddha.

Hinayana (Skt) — ཐེག་པ་དམན་པ། [T: thegs pa dman pa] *(thegpa menpa)*; Lesser Vehicle. Includes the first two yanas, the Shravakayana and Pratyekabuddhayana, whose fruition is individual liberation. NG

Ignorance of false imagination — ཀུན་བཏགས། [T: kun brtags] *(kun-tak)*; also translated both as the ignorance of labeling and as the ignorance of imputation.

Interdependent Origination — *See* Pratitya samutpada *and* Twelve nidanas.

Ishvaris — *See* Twenty-eight ishvaris.

Ji tawa — ཇི་ལྟ་བ། [T: ji lta ba]; the wisdom of seeing things as they are.

Ji nyepa — ཇི་སྙེད་པ། [T: ji snyed pa]; the wisdom of seeing things in their varieties and to their extent.

Jnana (Skt) — ཡེ་ཤེས། [T: ye shes] *(yeshe)*; wisdom.

Jö du mey pay jöpa — བརྗོད་དུ་མེད་པའི་བརྗོད་པ། [T: brjod du med pa'i brjod pa]; speechless speech.

Gyu ma ta bü ting nge dzin — སྒྱུ་མ་ལྟ་བུའི་ཏིང་ངེ་འཛིན། [T: sgyu ma lta bu'i ting nge 'dzin]; illusionlike samadhi.

Kadak — ཀ་དག [T: ka dak]; alpha-purity or primordially pure.

Kagyupas — བཀའ་བརྒྱུད་པ།[T: bka' brgyud pa]; followers of the Kagyu lineage, the lineage of oral instructions. The Kagyu lineage was brought to Tibet by Marpa Lotsawa in the eleventh century C.E.

Kaliyuga (Skt) — སྙིགས་དུས། [T: snyigs dus] *(nyik dü)*; the polluted age.

Karmapa — ཀརྨ་པ། [T: karma pa]; the head of the Karma Kagyu School of Tibetan Buddhism. The first Karmapa, Dusum Khyenpa, was a disciple of Gampopa. The current incarnation, His Holiness the Seventeenth Gyalwang Karmapa, Ogyen Thrinley Dorje, escaped from Tibet in January 2000. He currently resides in India.

Kriya Tantra (Skt) — The fourth yana in the nine-yana journey.

Kuntuzangmo — ཀུན་ཏུ་བཟང་མོ། [T: kun tu bzang mo]; consort of Kuntuzangpo. (Skt: Samantabhadri)

Kuntuzangpo — ཀུན་ཏུ་བཟང་པོ། [T: kun tu bzang po]; the primordial buddha in the Dzogchen tradition. (Skt: Samantabhadra)

Lhagtong — ལྷག་མཐོང་། [T: lhag mthong]; superior insight. (Skt: vipashyana)

Lhündrup — ལྷུན་གྲུབ། [T: lhun grub]; spontaneous presence. Refers to the fact that emptiness is not simply empty; it is also luminous. It has always been this way; this is not something that is or can be newly produced. It is the nature of things from the beginning. NG

Madhyamaka (Skt) — དབུ་མ། [T: dbu ma] (uma); the Middle Way. A philosophical school, founded by Nagarjuna, emphasizing emptiness.

Mahamudra (Skt) — ཕྱག་རྒྱ་ཆེན་པོ། [T: phyag rgya chen po] (chaggya chenpo); the Great Seal. The nature of mind as taught in the Kagyu tradition.

Mahasiddhas (Skt) — གྲུབ་ཐོབ་ཆེན་པོ། [T: grub thob chen po] (drubthob chen po); Vajrayana masters who have fully realized enlightenment. It generally refers to those whose outward manifestation is not limited to monasticism, but engage in apparently mundane activities as part of their manifestation.

Mahayana (Skt) — ཐེག་པ་ཆེན་པོ། [T: theg pa chen po] (thegpa chenpo); Greater Vehicle. The bodhisattva vehicle whose fruition is complete awakening. Includes the Paramitayana, based on the Sutra teachings, and the Vajrayana, or Secret Mantra, based on the tantras. Also known as the Bodhisattvayana. NG

Mahayoga (Skt) — Great union; it is the seventh yana in the nine-yana journey.

Manjushrimitra (Skt) — An Indian yogi; disciple of Garab Dorje and teacher of Sri Simha.

Ma rigpa — མ་རིག་པ། [T: ma rig pa]; ignorance.

Marpa — མར་པ། [T: mar pa]; also known as Marpa Lotsawa (Marpa the Translator). The principal disciple of Naropa and teacher of Milarepa. Marpa brought the Kagyu lineage from India to Tibet.

Milarepa — མི་ལ་རས་པ། [T: mi la ras pa]; one of the foremost disciples of Marpa Lotsawa and teacher of Gampopa. (1140-1123). NG. Milarepa was the personification of the renunciant yogi tradition.

Muni (Skt) — ཐུབ་པ། [T: thub pa] (thuppa); sage.

Nagarjuna (Skt) — གྲུ་སྒྲུབ། [T: klu sgrub] *(lu drub)*; Indian master of Madhya-maka philosophy. NG

Nalanda — The great monastic university in India destroyed by the Muslim invaders in the twelfth century C.E.

Naropa — Indian Mahasiddha, disciple of Tilopa and teacher of Marpa. (1016-1100). Naropa was an abbot of Nalanda before his studies with Tilopa.

Ngöndro — སྔོན་འགྲོ། [T: sngon 'gro]; preliminary practice. Ngöndro includes the ordinary preliminaries of the four reminders as well as the extraordi-nary preliminaries of the Vajrayana that include the accumulation prac-tices of refuge, prostration, Vajrasattva mantra, mandala offering, and guru yoga.

Nine-yana journey — The path to liberation according to the Dzogchen tra-dition.

Nirmanakaya (Skt) — སྤྲུལ་པའི་སྐུ། [T: sprul pa'i sku] *(trulpay ku)*; the form kaya of a buddha that can appear to both impure and pure beings. It is the fruition that is achieved for the benefit of sentient beings. It is also said that the mind, though free from arising and ceasing, manifests in various ways, so that it is the unceasing appearances of the expressive power of mind. NG. Human manifestation of the enlightened one, Shakyamuni Buddha.

Nirvana (Skt) — མྱ་ངན་ལས་འདས་པ། [T: mya ngan las 'das pa] *(nyangen le depa)*; pass beyond suffering. Can either mean the liberation, ཐར་པ། [T: thar pa] *(tharpa)*, from suffering achieved though the Shravakayana or the Pratyeka-buddhayana, or the state of omniscience, ཐམས་ཅད་མཁྱེན་པ། [T: thams cad mkhyen pa] *(thamche khyenpa)*, complete awakening, achieved through the Mahayana. NG. Nirvana is the experience of the absence of suffering and pain. It is the experience of the basic nature of mind.

Padmasambhava (Skt) — Vajrayana master who brought the Dzogchen teach-ings to Tibet in the eighth century C.E. Also known as Guru Rinpoche, he left hidden teachings to be found later for the benefit of future disciples. See also *Terma*.

Paramita (Skt) — ཕ་རོལ་ཏུ་ཕྱིན་པ། [T: pha rol tu phyin pa] *(pharol tu jinpa)*; transcendent perfection.

Prajna (Skt) — ཤེས་རབ། [T: shes rab] *(sherab)*; superior knowledge, insight.

Pratitya samutpada (Skt) — རྟེན་ཅིང་འབྲེལ་བར་འབྱུང་བ། [T: rten cing 'brel bar 'byung ba] *(tenching drelwar jungwa)*; the interconnectedness of all things, the fact that they arise in dependence on causes and conditions. NG

Pratyekabuddhayana (Skt) — རང་སངས་རྒྱས་རྐྱི་ཐེག་པ། [T: rang sangs rgyas rkyi theg pa] *(rang sanggye kyi thekpa)*; second yana in the nine-yana journey.

Primordial purity — *See* Kadak.

Prahadhani (Skt) — Mother of Garab Dorje.

Rahu or Rahula (Skt) — In the Dzogchen tantras, Rahula is a protector with thousands of eyes. In Tibetan astrology, eclipses are called Rahu.

Ratnasambhava — རིན་ཆེན་འབྱུང་གནས། [T: rin chen 'byung gnas] *(rinchen jungne)*; the buddha of the southern direction. *See* Five wisdoms.

Relative truth — ཀུན་རྫོབ་བདེན་པ། [T: kun rdzob bden pa] *(kundzop denpa)*.

Rigpa — རིག་པ། [T: rig pa]; naked awareness, bare awareness.

Rigpa rang-tshuk ma thup-pa — རིག་པ་རང་ཚུགས་མ་ཐུབ་པ། [T: rig pa rang tshugs ma thub pa]; rigpa has its own characteristics.

Rishi (Skt) — དྲང་སྲོང་། [T: drang srong] *(drang song)*; upright ones. Accomplished sages or meditators. NG

Sadhu (Skt) — ཏིང་ངེ་འཛིན་པ། [T: ting nge 'dzin pa] *(tingnre dzinpa)*; Indian yogi-ascetic.

Samadhi (Skt) — ཏིང་འཛིན། [T: ting 'dzin] *(tingdzin)*; meditative absorption or meditative stabilization.

Samantabhadra (Skt) — *See* Kuntuzangpo.

Samaya (Skt) — དམ་ཚིག [T: dam tshig] *(dam tsig)*; commitments of the Vajrayana path. NG

Sambhogakaya (Skt) — ལོངས་སྤྱོད་རྫོགས་པའི་སྐུ། [T: longs spyod rdzogs pa'i sku] (*longchö dzogpay ku*); the form kaya of a buddha adorned with the major and minor marks, which appears only to noble bodhisattvas. It is the fruition that is achieved for the benefit of other sentient beings. It is also said that it is the nonabiding of mind and the mind's awareness and clarity. NG. The meaning of sambhogakaya is the body of enjoyment. Here, enjoyment refers to yönten, the richness of sambhogakaya.

Samsara (Skt) — འཁོར་བ། [T: 'khor ba] (*khor wa*); cyclic existence. The state of existence, experienced by sentient beings due to their ignorance, in which suffering is the predominant experience. NG

Saraha (Skt) — Also known as the Great Brahmin. An Indian Mahasiddha and Mahamudra master. NG

Shakyamuni (Skt) — ཤཱཀྱ་ཐུབ་པ། [T: shakya thub pa] (*shakya thuppa*); the historical buddha.

Shamatha (Skt) — ཞི་གནས། [T: zhi gnas] (*shi-ney*); calm abiding meditation.

Shantideva (Skt) — ཞི་བ་ལྷ། [T: zhi ba lha] (*shiwa lha*); author of the *Bodhicarya-vatara, Entering the Middle Way.*

Shitro — ཞི་ཁྲོ། [T: zhi khro]; the peaceful and wrathful deities that appear in the bardo.

Shönnu bum-ku — གཞོན་ནུ་བུམ་སྐུ། [T: gzhon nu bum sku]; youthful buddha in a vase.

Shravakayana (Skt) — ཉན་ཐོས་ཀྱི་ཐེག་པ། [T: nyan thos kyi theg pa] (*nyenthö kyi thekpa*); first yana in the nine-yana journey, the path for practitioners who attain nirvana through practicing the first turning of the dharma wheel, the teachings of the Four Noble Truths. NG

Six Realms — འགྲོ་དྲུག [T: 'gro drug] (*dro drug*); the hell realm, hungry ghost realm, animal realm, human realm, asura or jealous gods' realm, and gods' realm.

Skandha (Skt) — ཕུང་པོ། [T: phung po] (*phungpo*); aggregates. The five skandhas are form, sensation, concept, formation, and consciousness. The Buddha taught that we misconceive the five skandhas as a single self.

Sri Simha (Skt) — དཔལ་གྱི་སེངྒེ། [T: dpal gyi seng ge] *(pelgyi sengge)*; a Chinese yogi who lived in India. Sri Simha was a disciple of Manjushrimitra and teacher of Padmasambhava.

Superimposition — སྒྲོ་འདོགས། [T: sgro 'dogs] *(dro dog)*; to take something to exist in a way that it does not, e.g., to ascribe true existence to something that does not have true existence. Also translated as "exaggerations." *See also* Denigration. NG

Sutrayana (Skt) — མདོའི་ཐེག་པ། [T: mdo'i theg pa] *(doyi thekpa)*; the path as taught by the Buddha in the sutras.

Svabhavakaya (Skt) — ངོ་བོ་ཉིད་སྐུ། [T: ngo bo nyid sku] *(ngo wo nyi ku)*; usually said to be the inseparability of the three kayas; also explained as the emptiness of mind. NG

Tantra of Penetrating Wisdom — དགོངས་པ་ཟང་ཐལ་གྱི་རྒྱུད། [T: dgongs pa zang thal gyi rgyud] *(gongpa zang-thal gyi gyü)*; alternatively, the *Tantra of Transcendent Intention*.

Tantrayana (Skt) — རྒྱུད་ཀྱི་ཐེག་པ། [T: rgyud kyi theg pa] *(gyü kyi thekpa)*; the path as taught by the Buddha in the tantras. *See also* Vajrayana.

Tendrel — རྟེན་འབྲེལ། [T: rten 'brel]; auspicious coincidence.

Terma — གཏེར་མ། [T: gter ma]; teachings hidden by Padmasambhava for the benefit of future disciples. These teachings are hidden by Padmasambhava to be discovered and taught after his death by tertons, who are those who find termas. These teachings are said to be hidden so that they will be found when they are most useful in future times of difficulty.

Thamal gyi shepa — ཐ་མལ་གྱི་ཤེས་པ། [T: tha mal gyi shes pa]; ordinary mind. The nature of mind according to the Mahamudra tradition.

Thögal — ཐོད་རྒལ། [T: thod rgal]; direct crossing. The Dzogchen practice emphasizing spontaneous presence.

Three realms — ཁམས་གསུམ། [T: khams gsum] *(kham sum)*; includes the desire realm, འདོད་ཁམས། [T: 'dod khams] *(dö kham)*; the form realm, གཟུགས་ཁམས། [T: gzugs khams] *(zug kham)*; and the formless realm, གཟུགས་མེད་ཁམས། [T: gzugs med khams] *(zug mey kham)*.

Tilopa — Indian Mahasiddha, teacher of Naropa. (988-1069). NG. First human holder of the Kagyu lineage. He received teachings directly from Vajradhara, primordial buddha of the Mahamudra tradition.

Tonglen — གཏོང་ལེན། [T: gtong len]; "sending and taking"; a method for developing bodhicitta

Tramen — See Eight tramen.

Transmission — Realization of enlightenment taught by master to disciple in an unbroken line.

Trekchö — ཁྲེགས་ཆོད། [T: khregs chod]; the Dzogchen practice of cutting through.

Trülpa — འཁྲུལ་པ། [T: 'khrul pa]; delusion; confusion; mistakenness.

Twelve nidanas (Skt) — རྟེན་འབྲེལ་བཅུ་གཉིས། [T: rten 'brel bcu gnyis] (ten drel chu nyi); also known as the twelve links of interdependent origination.

Twenty-eight ishvaris (Skt) — དབང་ཕྱུག་མ་ཉེར་བརྒྱད། [T: dbang phyug ma nyer brgyad] (wangchukma); wrathful emanations of the four female gate keepers among the forty-two peaceful deities. Seven for each of the four activities.

Uddiyana (Skt) — ཨོ་རྒྱན། [T: o rgyan] (ogyen/urgyen); northwest of India, birthplace of Garab Dorje and Padmasambhava. It is said to be located in present day Afghanistan.

Upa Tantra (Skt) — The fifth yana in the nine-yana journey.

Vairochana (Skt) — རྣམ་པར་སྣང་མཛད། [T: rnam par snang mdzad] (nampar nangdze); the buddha of the central direction.

Vajrasattva (Skt) — A sambhogakaya buddha. Vajrasattva transmitted the Dzogchen teachings to Garab Dorje. See Dorje Sempa.

Vajrayana (Skt) — རྡོ་རྗེ་ཐེག་པ། [T: rdo rje theg pa] (dorje thegpa); the Tantric teachings of the Mahayana. It is the short path, ཉེ་ལམ། [T: nye lam] (nye lam), that utilizes a variety of methods that take the results of awakening as the path. Also called Secret Mantra, Mantrayana, Tantrayana, or the resultant vehicle, འབྲས་བུའི་ཐེག་པ། [T: 'bras bu'i theg pa] (dre bui theg pa).

Vipashyana — *See* Lhagthong.

Ying-rik — དབྱིངས་རིག [T: dbyings rig]; space and wisdom.

Yidak — ཡི་དྭགས། [T: yi dwags]; tortured spirits, hungry ghosts.

Yidam — ཡི་དམ། [T: yi dam]; meditation deity.

Yönten — ཡོན་ཏན། [T: yön tan]; qualities.